Last Dance for Grace

The Crystal Mangum Story

By Crystal Mangum

with

Vincent Clark

fire! Books
Los Angeles & Raleigh

© 2008

Last Dance for Grace: The Crystal Mangum Story

fire! Books

Published by fire! Films and Books
Fire! Films and Books, Inc., Raleigh, NC

Copyright © 2008 by fire! Books

All rights reserved. No part of this book may be reproduced, scanned, or distributed in any form (printed or electronic) without permission. Please do not violate this copyright. Participating in or encouraging piracy of this copyrighted material is a violation of the rights of the author and publisher. Please only purchase only authorized editions. This edition is also available as an e-book. Published simultaneously in Canada and U.K.

Mangum, Crystal, 2008
Last Dance for Grace / Crystal Mangum

ISBN 9-78098178372-7

Printed in the United States of America

Edited by Louise Stone

Designed by Carla deBose

This work is based on true events. Names, places and incidents are the best recollections of the author. Some of the names have been changed to protect individuals who have requested anonymity or could not be contacted.

Table of Contents

Foreword	v
Introduction	1
Meeting	18
March 2006	32
Family	56
Unravel	68
Rebellion	84
Meeting the Devil	100
Rocking the Boat	142
Taxi Ride	166
March 13, 2006—Part 2	188
Case Closed	208
New Beginning	219
Epilogue	231

Dedication

I dedicate this book to my three children: Richard, Arianna, and Kayla.

— *Crystal G. Mangum*

Foreword

Trial by? ...

This is a story about justice. If we strip away our opinions about exotic dancers, escorts, and for this matter, even our opinions about lacrosse players, the predominant concern should be about how the infamous Duke Lacrosse case has been handled. Who was the judge and who was the jury?

We live in an American culture that says it values equity, fairness, and justice. But, in essence, the behaviors that the culture condones are inconsistent with the espoused value system. Equity, in the Duke Lacrosse case, would appear as both accuser and accused having access to the same level of quality legal representation. I know this did not happen. It would look like both accused and accuser were being treated fairly in the media portrayals. In my opinion, this did not happen. Finally, it would look like the accused rapists and the accuser were being apprised equally of all the information and decisions regarding the case. Again, I feel certain this did not happen.

One of the first questions Crystal Mangum, the accuser in this case, remembers receiving from the district attorney's office was, "Do you have an attorney?" An assault victim with an attorney? I do not think most victims are prepared with their own counsel. I suppose I genuinely think too much like a humanist. Even so, my question was, "Why would a *victim* need an attorney?"

As the media circus surrounding the case played more and more on the six o'clock news, I began to see why it would be necessary for a victim to need legal representation. The media, the district attorney's office, the tabloids, and parasites of all kinds were after the accuser. Even so, how could this be? I had always heard about victims' rights. Would those sworn to serve and protect do so for the rights of the victim? Not!

After experiencing sexual assault, many women often feel confused and lonely. Their ability to trust is usually zapped. Self-esteem suffers greatly. Women, sometimes slip into a place where they question themselves and wonder, "Did I cause this to happen to me?" After experiencing this type of personal violation, women can become extremely fragile. In some cases, sexual assault is the breaking point. Repeated attacks can be even more crushing to the psyche. Some women never recover. There are, however, more of us who bounce back and live fulfilling lives.

So let us go back to the woman who is broken after being assaulted. Her logic may be hampered. Her judgment may be skewed. Yet, she still must contend with the constant, whirlwind swirling of questions and public ridicule. Public ridicule? Should I even know the victim's name so early in the investigation? Aren't their laws that protect the victim?

After short reflection, I am convinced that yes, this woman needs legal representation. Especially when she has accused those who are being represented by boys from the million-dollar club. I can only imagine that every word out of the accused mouths was orchestrated. They were thoroughly coached and advised about how to handle themselves during this time, which is what a good attorney should do for his client. On the other hand, there was no one "real" there for the accuser. Real defines an entity who has no ulterior motives.

The accuser could not afford the kind of legal representation the Duke players could afford. Face it. The Friends of Duke raised millions to assist the Duke players with their defense. Who was going to help the exotic dancer raise money for her legal representation? She was dancing to provide for her family. It seems reasonable that she would not have the kind of money to match the Friends' efforts.

Change gears for a second and ask some disturbing questions. If an exotic dancer is raped while on the job, are we less likely to find her testimony credible on account of the type of work, she does? Is she judged by the same standards as the prim church girl? Do we assume the exotic dancer is "asking for it," just because she earns money by using her body as an entertainment tool? Back to the age-old question of do we judge the woman more harshly than the man? Can men get off freely, such as the lacrosse players, with a mere excuse of "We exercised poor judgment?" If an exotic dancer is promiscuous and sleeps with five or six guys within a twenty-four-hour time period, do we find her less credible if she says that the seventh guy raped her? These are questions that everyone must answer for him or her self.

When I heard that North Carolina Attorney General Roy Cooper proclaim emphatically the Duke players as innocent, I was floored. I knew then that some of my disturbing questions had not been deeply considered. I knew then that Crystal's lack of legal representation had hurt her immensely.

According to a Fox news report on April 11, 2007: "The result of our review and investigation shows clearly that there is insufficient evidence to proceed on any of the charges," Cooper said. "Today we are filing notices of dismissal for all charges."

He further added: "We believe these cases were a result of a tragic rush to accuse and failure to verify serious allegations. Based on these significant inconsistencies of evidence and the various accounts given by the accusing witness, we believe these three individuals are innocent of these charges." Cooper said not only are the players innocent of the charges they faced, but also there is "no credible evidence that an attack occurred at that house on that night."

Wow! He called them innocent. Consequently, what does that make the accuser? Is he aware of the state's definition of assault?

According to Cooper, "Our investigators looked at the records, and we think she may have believed the stories she was telling." Cooper further explained, "We believe it's in the best interest of justice not to bring charges." Whose best interest, Mr. Cooper?

One of my old professors would often remind me to question: Under what conditions? To whom does this apply? Who will benefit from this situation as it is currently stated? So, I ask, in this case, whose best interest is being served? Whose justice? From the outside looking in, the best interest of the victim has never been a priority. It appears that from the very beginning, ulterior motives clouded the truth. We know that the victim has still not experienced justice. Her story has never been heard. We have only experienced second-hand interpretations of her saga.

This case has been reduced to a scene after scene of lawsuits about everything but the victim's experience, to page after page of Internet speculation, and finally to interview after interview dominated by "he said, she said." Finally, we are at place where you, the outsiders, become up close and personal with Crystal Mangum.

Before you jump into this story, I encourage you to consider a few things. Our perceptions are based on how we have lived and on how we have interpreted each event in our lives. We rely on all of our senses to gather information about our surrounding environments. From the information we gain, we try to make sense of the world around us. I have always been befuddled as to how some people can find wrong in others and overlook their own individual shortcomings. This type of one-sided analysis yields a dangerous conclusion.

I remember reading Nathaniel Hawthorne's "The Scarlet Letter" in my teen years. The story intrigued me then and now it seems immensely relevant to the one-sided analysis of the Duke Lacrosse case. The plot of Hawthorne's novel is built around the sin committed by two people; however, the sin is made more voluminous in scope by an entire religious group's judgment of these two sinners and their sin. The equation presented by the plot leans toward a hypocritical outcome. Hypocrisy is present in instances where people use the Bible as the tool of persecution; nevertheless, they go against the Bible's teaching in their acts of persecution. Beyond a doubt, the act of persecuting in and of itself is hypocritical.

Hawthorne's entire book represents several lessons regarding persecution, judging, and labeling. Like the Duke case, Hawthorne's female character is judged harsher than the male characters. Look at the nature of judging and how it ostracizes and makes the reader feel lonely. Read further in this text and you will see how a woman struggling to provide for her children and dedicated to providing better for them and for herself has been shunned because she—not the society's perfect woman specimen—chose to speak out against sexual abuse.

In "The Scarlet Letter" the Puritan community of 17th-century Boston was aggressive in eradicating sin and crimes such as adultery. Publicly, the Puritan women carried themselves in an exemplary fashion. They appeared to be upstanding wives and mothers—unlike what they saw when they looked at Hester Prynne, who was estranged from her husband yet was with child. The Puritan example parallels the American women's general disdain for exotic dancers and the like. Oddly, this same group relaxes its disdain and finds tolerance for those in the dancers' audiences. Here we begin to see the bias more clearly and can call it for what it is—hypocrisy.

Pornography, prostitution, and erotica tend to cause negative perceptions of the worker-participants in these situations. Similarly, the Puritan community not only regarded adultery as a sin, but had also criminalized the act. The women seemed hardest on Hester. There was no sense of empathy, no sense of, "I've been there, and I know how lonely and cold nights can get."

Like the community response in Hawthorne's novel, the Duke Lacrosse case made national headlines. This was no longer a campus incident. It was national call to decide if these young athletes could possibly be guilty of a sexual assault on an exotic dancer. Women in the novel and many women who discussed the Duke case tended to be very judgmental of other women's moral conduct. I know women who call exotic dancers whores, but who find their own penchant to only sleep with BMW-driving, well-dressed, white-collar, college graduates who pay their bills as a simple act of self-preservation.

Again we resort back to one's perception. Persecution or judgment seems most harsh when it comes from one of your own. Hester would probably have had a greater sense of self-worth had the women been more understanding about her situation. Instead of further debasing her, the Puritan women had the power to elevate Hester. The purpose not being to praise her for her sin, but to let her know that she was not alone. Crystal Mangum was alone dealing with the madness of this national attention and the madness of this *public* trial.

Because there has been no legal trial, this case has been tried in the public eye. You and I have been and are the judges.

When judging, we heap our values and morals on others. We close the door to learning about others and cut off the faucet of meaningful relationships. Although Hester was an adulteress, that did not make her any less human. Although Crystal was an exotic dancer, that does not make her any less human.

There was no need for the town to make a public spectacle of Hester; however, they did. There was no need for the media to make a public spectacle of Crystal, but they tried. Who benefited from these public expositions? What was gained? Maybe the Puritans felt more pious when they judged deeds and put sinners to shame. Maybe they thought that their actions towards Hester would curtail adultery in the town. Maybe they even thought that calling attention to Hester's sin would take attention away from their own sins. Even so, what would we as a contemporary public benefit from belittling an assault victim? For some, the parade of lawsuits is a benefit. For others, the benefit question still looms.

Judging, which is manifest by labeling, has created some of the major problems in our schools and communities today. Policemen, teachers, salespeople, and a gamut of others often judge individuals based on the color of their skin, the price of their clothes, and even by the music they listen to. This is incredibly unfair and limits individuality. Judging often perpetuates a negative sense of self for the individual being judged as will be illustrated by the narrative in this text. The individual being judged is not valued by those who are doing the judging, which leads the person being judged to believe herself to be an aberration or a deviant person.

The hypocrisy of judging or labeling has led to major societal catastrophes such as slavery and the holocaust. It has been hundreds of years since these incidents were prevalent, but the repercussions still exist. High crime rates, increased unemployment, and hate crimes are a result of institutionalized judging. If the children of today are to be prepared for the challenges of the future, they need to work and play in an environment that promotes diversity. Unfortunately, we cannot break the spell cast by unfair labeling or judging as easily as Hawthorne did in "The Scarlet Letter." We can, however, promote individuality and tolerance by embracing those who are different than ourselves. It is okay to voice one's own opinion. On the other hand, it is not okay to ostracize, ridicule, or publicly humiliate an individual because her views, morals, and/or values differ from our own.

The hypocrisy of labeling and judging has caused tremendous heartache for many. The only way to mitigate the heartache is for society to be more tolerant and less judgmental. For the religious community, let the Supreme Being judge. For municipalities, let the courts judge. For the sake of mankind, "judge ye not that ye be judged not."

— *Myra M. Shird, Ph.D.*

Communications, Women's Studies, and Social Advocacy professor, and textbook author of "Communication Voices," "The Fundamentals of Speech Communication," and "The Quilt: Cultural Voices"

Introduction

I got a call from a longtime friend. He is an attorney and knew about everything going on with high profile legal cases in North Carolina. He was especially aware of controversial cases that had to do with civil rights issues. My friend is probably one if the best civil rights lawyers in the country and has done so much to see that justice is done for those who have the deck stacked against them. We talked often because there was always some case that we could commiserate over.

No matter how far we had come on civil rights in America, too many people were still getting the "short end of the stick" when in court. Money and a competent defense attorney are priceless in any court. Consequently, I fully expected this call was about another situation that needed the public's attention. The reason he was calling me that day would catch me totally off guard. He said he believed he could arrange a meeting with the accuser in the Duke Lacrosse case.

"Is she at your house?" I asked. "Do you know her?"

"No, she's not here, but I know someone I can put you in touch with who knows her. Give me a few days and let me see what I can do."

My heart pounded. I had been waiting for the opportunity to meet the accuser. The case had been constantly on my mind. For some reason I felt as though I needed to know her. I needed to know as much as I could. I had been troubled about the entire thing, since first hearing and reading about it. I slept uneasily every night, and I wasn't going to rest until I discovered what really happened.

Not only had the Duke Lacrosse case become a fixture on the local news, but it had also found a life on cable television, the Internet, and I am sure there were people outside of the country who had heard of the case. I mentioned to my friend at least a dozen times that I felt compelled to meet the accuser. I knew it was going to be an important moment in the history of the state of North Carolina, but I never imagined the impact it would have around the country. If anyone could set up such a meeting, I knew my friend could. He was a crusading attorney who wanted to make sure that men and women who had been wrongly convicted got a fair shake. In the cases where he could make a difference, he fought for exoneration. I believed in that too. I still do.

To be wrongly accused and convicted must be an incredibly helpless feeling. I had been working for months with a mother in Knightdale, North Carolina, to free her sons who had been convicted of rape. They were poor, black, and had below average IQ's. Their written and signed confessions were impossible since neither could read or write. I had hit a stonewall in that case and was growing more frustrated everyday. Not a single person was interested in what I had found.

Reading the trial transcripts, DNA and police reports made it appear to be a case for the convicted men to be exonerated. Alas, that would prove to be an impossible task since not a soul who could willingly help reopen the case wanted to have anything to do with it.

Knowing what I knew about the case in Knightdale made me all the more curious about the Duke Lacrosse case. I was intrigued because a narrative had developed demonstrating that the prosecutor was unfairly treating the defendants in the case. I believed that if any case had been unfair it certainly wasn't the Duke case. The case that needed the light shown on it was the Knightdale case. Instead, the Duke case was the most public circus, besides the OJ trial, that I could remember in my 43 years.

I knew district attorneys sent people to jail and even to the death house with faulty or manufactured evidence. We were hearing that it was happening in this case as well, but something told me this was different. I was skeptical and believed that if I could at least talk to the accuser, I would see that the truth was not as clear-cut as the defense lawyers would have us believe.

My lawyer friend and I wondered aloud about how the investigation was being handled and whether everything was out in the open. I know we both were concerned that the defense and the accuser may not have been treated fairly. No one could argue that having Sean Hannity and others talking about the case nightly was helping the cause of justice. It added to the confusion and made certain that the case would become noteworthy and newsworthy for all the wrong reasons.

Being a black man, I was especially sensitive and considered myself a well-read student of history. I had studied North Carolina history and remembered one case in particular. Even though it had happened 100 years ago, it was the start of a series of lynchings in North Carolina and throughout the South that would last well into the 1960s. Two black men in Danbury, Stokes County, were lynched on the same night for "outraging a prominent white woman." It sounded so quaint and Victorian to say "outraged," but just what exactly was that? What I do know is that neither man had a chance to go to a trial, and even if they had, hanging in the town square would have been their likely punishment. The only difference is that the state of North Carolina would have officially sanctioned the killing.

White men had likely committed the same kind of outrage on black women for at least a good portion of America's history. Few if any of those men suffered a lynching let alone a courtroom trial. Someone wanted us to believe that the Duke defendants were suffering something akin to a lynching, but I just could not buy it. North Carolina was not immune to unfairly prosecuting poor men. I just could not comprehend how having Joe Cheshire as your lawyer was being put at a disadvantage.

After I hung up the phone I thought back to how I heard about the case. I could remember so clearly the moment as I sat in the waiting area at Midway Airport wanting desperately to be somewhere else. I had been hoping to get on an earlier flight back to Raleigh but there were no seats available, so I had to sit for a few hours. I was tired because I had been traveling a lot, and I was spending many more hours in airports than I wanted.

Right then, the only thing I could think about was being home. Out of all the places I have ever been, North Carolina seemed the right place for me. I don't know if other people feel this way but there is something really special about North Carolina. I suppose people who live in other places say that about where they live. The truth is I am a country boy at heart and the city can only hold my attention for a short while.

Being in Chicago for a few days was a good time but after a while the constant noise got to me. I wanted to get back into a quiet environment where there was nothing going on. A place where there wasn't constant movement, where people took things easy, and where the pace is slower. As I sat there staring out the window at the tarmac, I thought that the best thing about North Carolina is how sane things are there.

Don't get me wrong. North Carolina is not some idyllic place like Mayberry. It is the tenth most-populated state and growing and never was exactly like Andy and Barney portrayed it. Even so, there is something different about it. The cities and towns in the state make it such an appealing place that you feel like it is populated by Aunt Bea and Otis—cities like Raleigh, Durham, and Charlotte are straining under the pressures of rapid growth because people want that lifestyle they believe exists here. However, with that rapid growth comes many bad things and chief among them are crime and safety issues.

Durham suffers from an image problem when people discuss crime. I overhear conversations of people talking about crime in Durham as if they were speaking of Philadelphia or Newark. Yes, there are murders, rapes, and other mayhem but nothing on the scale of what I saw when I traveled away from home.

I will argue that Durham gets an incredibly bad rap within North Carolina and now probably from outside. I hear people all the time saying how they wouldn't want to go to downtown Durham, but they do—all the time. The center of the city has been converted to a thriving retail and entertainment center. The Durham Bulls play in one of the best ballparks in the country, major or minor league, and are sold out much of the time.

However, the *au courant* thing to say around your friends is that you wouldn't be caught doing anything in

Durham. Race has a lot to do with the image of Durham. Just like it does with Detroit and Newark, and used to with Washington, DC, before it was gentrified. Cities with significant black populations and where black coalitions can have meaningful political clout tend to have "urban" problems like crime. On account of the large black population—about 43 percent of the total—Durham gets special scrutiny. It also has a growing Spanish-speaking minority that affects whites becoming a minority by a slim margin. Politically speaking, that allows Durham to elect a black mayor. It has also led to many contentious city council meetings and school board debates over the last few decades because a conservative block can no longer put together the numbers needed to elect their candidates.

None of that mattered to me right then because I was still in Chicago, but over the next two years I would constantly think about Durham and how it is perceived. Right then, there was going to be a great deal of time to kill because I had gotten to the airport so early. Glancing up at the television playing CNN, it seemed as though I had already been here 100 times before. The stories seemed to repeat time and time again. I couldn't even tell you what any of the images were and everything seemed to be a blur. The constant chatter of the other waiting passengers drowned out the newsreaders anyway. There was something about Iraq. Blah, blah, blah... Something about Bush, blah, blah... That's about as much as I can tell you about what I saw.

I thought what I always think when I'm sitting in an airport on a hard plastic chair watching this stuff on the monitor: "The world is a screwed up place!" You start to wonder why there is always so much bad stuff going on. There is always some person missing somewhere like Natalie Holloway or a controversy like Don Imus and the "nappy headed hoes" comments to keep the cable channels going. Plus, there is always Paris Hilton to cover, if it is a really slow news cycle. Consequently, I cannot remember now what any of the stories were about but it really does not matter, as they might as well all have been the same regurgitation.

After the first half hour, the television was too much for me to take. Plus I was tired of listening in on inane conversations going on around me. I did not know any of the people anyway. Even though we were all waiting to go back to Raleigh-Durham, the other passengers might as well have been from anywhere. Even if I knew what they were talking about it would not change my life one bit.

Eventually, I did overhear someone say something about Duke and lacrosse. Then later on someone else mentioned something about Duke. My ears perked up. I hated anything related to Duke sports but not the people or the university. Everyone in the area picks a team to root against. Mine just happened to be the Blue Devils. Those passengers could not have possibly been talking about anything I wanted to know.

There was no alternative; I pulled out my laptop. What did we do before we had these things? Maybe we did not need them previously because we did not sit around airports as much. Even though I am often one of them now, people on laptops in public places bother me. It is the same feeling about on cell phones. Something about it seems pretentious. Surely, I was working on some important presentation or making some kind of deal. Even so, how much work could you really be doing anyway? The airport is the single most uncomfortable place in the world besides the plane itself and it is difficult to concentrate there. I rarely if ever took my laptop out for that very reason but this was the right time.

The truth is you mainly surf the Internet and look at all of the same crap you would look at if you were just staring up at the airport television monitor. The difference is you can select the junk you want to look at yourself and not have it handpicked by some producer in New York. So, I looked earnest and hard working as I put in my password. I did what always do. I logged on to the Web site for *The Raleigh News & Observer*. I suppose I could have looked at one of the local television Web sites but from my very early experience with the Internet *The News & Observer, The N&O,* had almost always been the first Web site I would open. I wasn't looking for anything in particular, but I felt that if I could just see what was going on back home, I might feel a little better.

As I studied the articles, one in particular caught my attention. I gravitated to it more on account of the byline,

Anne Blythe. Anne had edited a column I wrote at *The Chapel Hill News*. We had gotten along well and she rarely if ever changed anything I wrote. She was also willing to let me write about whatever I wanted and that is always good if you are a columnist. Most of the stuff she had written was good, and I always thought she was a fair reporter. Anne had written an article with someone named Samiha Khanna. I couldn't say whether I remembered ever reading anything written by Khanna but there were four words in the first sentence of the piece that stood out: rape, Duke University, party. That must have been what those waiting passengers were talking about.

My eyes diverted back to the headline. It was something like "Dancer Gives Details of Ordeal." Apparently, I had missed some big news. What dancer were they talking about and what kind of ordeal had she gone through? Were they saying that someone was raped at a party at Duke University? Maybe Durham was a bad place to be after all, and I was just deluding myself about how nothing crazy ever really happens. All of a sudden, I had a sick and uneasy feeling.

Rape and sexual assaults do not tend to get that kind of coverage early in the case. Surely, the investigation could not have been completed. The headline and the first sentences in the story made me assume that something horrible had happened. Just those few words prompted me to want to know more. My other immediate thought was that if students at Duke University were being accused of some crime, any crime, there was going to be a lot more said about it. I had in my mind that Duke students were somehow different than other college kids. Not for any reason other than that is what we tend to do. We ascribe traits to everyone based on our perceptions of the reputation of the institution to which they belong. Like football players from certain schools are considered dumb and criminals. It does not matter whether it was true or not. It is how we think.

I did not recall knowing anything about this news item. I would have remembered there being allegations of rape when I left for Chicago earlier in the week. At the time, I was preoccupied with my own agenda and trying to keep my head above economic water. Nevertheless, this would surely be something I needed to investigate. I have co-hosted a radio show in the Raleigh-Durham market for over 10 years, covering every topic you could imagine. This was likely to be on people's radar.

Reading further, the story turned ugly quickly. A young woman who was trying to work her way through college and take care of her two children was dancing for money at a party for about 40 Duke Lacrosse players. Dancing for any number of people struck me as an awful way to make a living. Besides that, it did not seem like the safest way to make a living. Immediately, I made an assumption about what happened, and I had not even read through half of the article. I needed to slow down and get to the end of the piece.

I could not stop thinking about this girl dancing her way through school. Surely, a college student dancing her way through college was just a cliché in the first place. Wasn't that just a stock character from some movie? Nobody really did that, did they? The truth is I had never seen a real live stripper perform in my life. I just never found myself in a position to experience something like that. What I knew about stripping and exotic dancing was strictly from the movies. I had always imagined the women who danced like that for a living were either drug abusers, prostitutes, or wannabe porn actresses. For a split second, I thought that perhaps it might have been her fault that she had been raped. She should have been home with her kids. I did not believe there were people who wanted to finish college and take care of their kids doing stuff like that in the first place. Then my good sense took over. I should not be prejudging anyone yet. According to the article, she was only trying to make ends meet so I needed to give her the benefit of the doubt.

There was little detail about the alleged assault. It was a rape case, and it had only been about a week since it happened. The whole thing must have traumatized the victim. That *The N&O* would even be interviewing an alleged victim so soon after the incident happened struck me as odd. I wondered why the media was not giving the victim time to deal with what had happened in the first place? Perhaps I was missing something, but it seemed to me that the reporting and editorial decision to run the story with its headline was a poor choice and inflammatory. I couldn't think of another time when *The N&O* had gone to such lengths to do a story about a rape victim, but I suppose there had never been one where the Duke lacrosse team was involved.

As I read on, I was even more convinced the paper was premature. The police were still looking for people to come forward. The Durham Police were constantly criticized for being ineffective in comparison to the other police departments in the area. Whether or not the criticism was deserved, they were getting it regularly. I was also positive that because Duke University's name appeared in the article, they were not going to sit on the sidelines and allow the reputation of Duke to be sullied. I figured there were already people associated with Duke making sure that this would be handled one way or another to protect Duke.

Further along in the article I felt my heart race. It seems that some of the people at this party had hurled racial epithets at the woman who had been raped. According to the reporter, a neighbor named Jason Bissey talked about all the commotion going on and the yelled racial epithets: "Thank your grandpa for my cotton T-shirt!" That made me angry. I could feel my temperature rise. I felt mad and hot because those epithets meant the woman was black and the people accused of hurting her were likely white.

The specter of racism hanging over the story bothered me. If anything got people riled up, it would be race and sex together. Americans cannot even discuss the subjects individually. When the two are put together you have the makings of a very contentious issue. Race introduced into any discussion is a stick of dynamite.

It was so clear to me at the time that *The N&O* in its zeal to tell the rape victims' side of things made a serious editorial lapse and allowed some very inflammatory stuff to run in the first story. It is not to say that withholding some of the key elements of the story would have made it less inflammatory in the end. I believe that no matter what had been said the attorneys for the accused players would have used some of the same tactics to have the players exonerated. What *The N&O* should have done is printed the incident as straight news right from the police blotter or not run the story at all until more police investigation had occurred. Attempting to talk to an alleged rape victim so soon after the incident hampered the truth search. Immediately people wanted to take sides. I know I was picking a side as I read the article.

The N&O is a responsible and good newspaper the majority of the time and has every right to run whatever news stories it chooses. I cannot imagine them ever again printing the kind of headlines they did in this case. Obviously there was no way that anyone could predict the level of interest in the case but that early article by *The N&O* unleashed a firestorm that has yet to be fully extinguished.

I had to remind myself that just because someone had made racist statements did not mean they had raped someone. What it did suggest to me was that there were first-class jerks involved, and it was going to be hard for me to give them the benefit of doubt. I am not so naive as to believe that there is no racism. I have been called a nigger more times than I care to remember. I've also personally experienced enough slights that sometimes I have to fight the urge that makes me want to cast all white people as racist.

Even so, I know it takes all kinds of people to make up the world, whether or not we like their attitudes. I did want the jerks yelling about cotton T-shirts to be called out. I wanted whoever assaulted this woman to be found and dealt with. Not that I was going to take an active role in the process of finding out what really happened myself, I did not know the woman and could not care less about that party with 40 of the Duke Lacrosse players.

My eyes darted across the page, and I read and reread the story a few more times. I was tempted to pull out my cell phone and call some people to ask what they knew about this, but I didn't. It was just one story about one woman after all. I was likely to never know her or much about what really happened. We all see cases every day that we have opinions about, but we don't know the people. After all, who really knows OJ or Phil Specter? We believe we do but that is just what we see in the media. I read through the rest of the news, but I could not really concentrate. This was going to be interesting.

On the flight back to Raleigh, a certain image played over and over again in my head. I saw some smug young white kid taunting some poor bedraggled stripper because she did not perform up to his standards. It did not say that in the article but that is how I imagined it. Everyone has his or her own reality no matter what the paper states. Each person's perspective and past go into painting a picture of what they believe happened. I had a feeling that most people were not going to take the side of the stripper on account of what they perceived she did for money. *She somehow deserved what was coming to her.* I even thought that for a minute. Of course others would not believe it because they were good boys from good families going to a good school. *If it had been black football players, then maybe it would make sense. Those guys got in trouble all the time. Why would some good white kid want to be with some black stripper anyway?*

My feelings were being driven by my problem with the idea of black women stripping for a room full of rowdy, drunk white boys in the first place. Perhaps they wanted more than a dance and were refused? I considered how society sexualizes black women. There is a whole genre of pornography that deals with interracial sex and the humiliation of black women. The idea of a white man abusing some black prostitute has appeal for some folk. Other white men consider black women there to be used, easily accessed, so it goes, and it has been that way since the first enslaved Africans came to America.

Even so, I didn't want to go there. Sometimes, black folks take 400 years of oppression and view everything through that lens. It is difficult not to process that way when you have lived the life of most black people in this country. Elements of this story that have to do with race are truly unsettling and uncomfortable. However, those same elements of race and sex hit a raw nerve in me. I tried not to think about it anymore and pushed aside these thoughts for a day or two.

The Durham police force was on the case. Someone was bound to come around and tell what happened, and it would be handled like any other court case. I could not imagine what would happen in the intervening 24 months. The victim in the case got a name, Crystal Mangum. The state of North Carolina would take over and say that the accused players were innocent of all charges. The District Attorney Mike Nifong would be disbarred and sent to jail for one day. The most unexpected twist for me is that I would end up being a part of the story. On that flight back to Raleigh-Durham, I never envisioned meeting the accuser. It was a rape case, after all, and the victim would never be identified.

Instead I got that unexpected phone call from my friend and within days I was sitting across a big conference table at a law office in downtown Durham.

Meeting

Before Crystal walked in the room, I imagined she would be like a streetwalker or hooker in an episode from some 1970's crime drama: Streetwise, chewing gum, and popping bubbles when she talked. Instead, in walked a very small woman. Perhaps she was no bigger than 5'1" and 100 pounds. After I got to know her, and when we were in the mall looking for clothes, I realized she was a size zero. Occasionally she had to buy clothes in the kids' section. Because of the ruckus the case generated, I had always pictured her being so much taller and fuller. Besides being shocked by how small she was, I was also taken aback when she opened her mouth to speak. She talked deliberately and spoke clearly.

"Crystal, how can I help you?" I asked.

She was definitely uncomfortable but looked directly at me. I knew she was suspicious of me and probably everyone she had encountered since the incident. By the time we met, the case had fallen apart completely. There were people trying to make money from her story. Plus, the defense lawyers and a group of right-wing bloggers had spent nearly a year on a campaign smearing her. There was not one positive thing I had seen or read about this woman, and she had no way of knowing if I believed what I had read about her.

"I just want people to know the truth."

I tried to keep eye contact; I wanted to gain her trust. "What is the truth, Crystal?"

In a strong clear voice she answered. "I'm not who they say I am. I'm not lying. Something did happen to me."

From that moment I believed something had happened, too. This person sitting in front of me was supposed to be delusional. I had met plenty of people like that and this person did not strike me that way. As we talked and she became more comfortable with me, I realized that she had been paying close attention to the news coverage. She knew which talk show hosts had said what and understood the politics of her case.

During that meeting we agreed to see each other as often as we could. The goal, from the beginning, was to get her side of the story out. Not a single newspaper or network tried to do any investigation after the defense attorneys began swaying public opinion. This was going to be more than difficult because I did not want this to become a story about specific people who had been charged. This had to be about Crystal and what she had experienced. At this point it did not matter who did what and exactly how they did it because the attorney general and the North Carolina Bar had made their point. The criminal case was closed, and it would serve no purpose to fight that. Nevertheless, it was and still is important to tell Crystal's side of the story.

The first few meetings with Crystal were difficult for me. She answered without hesitation all of the questions I asked. Never once did she seem to be hiding anything about her past or that night in March 2006. What bothered me the most is that there was this completely different person being described on the blogs and television and not the person sitting in front of me. Crystal could talk about news events, politics, and sophisticated concepts in psychology. I learned early on that she was not just some B-average student as many Internet rumors were reporting. She was carrying a nearly 3.7 GPA when the case broke. What exactly was going on? Who were these people who spent their time trying to defame Crystal? If I had not been meeting with her, I would have expected that she could barely hold her head up straight. I certainly didn't expect her to be one of the best students in her department.

I have met plenty of famous and high profile people, and plenty of manipulators as well. Crystal seemed as ordinary as you could be.

I needed to square the two portraits of this woman. As difficult as it was, I read as many of the blogs as I could. It appeared that that is where the news media was getting most of its information anyway. Sean Hannity made constant tirades against Crystal. I began to notice that most of his rants were identical to people such as Internet columnists Michael Gaynor, Stuart Taylor, and K.C. Johnson. I found it amazing that these non-local people invested so much time and energy on the case. Most people I talked with just wanted the case resolved as fairly as possible.

From the time the case became public and until the day I began writing this book, an attempt was being made to craft a narrative of the Duke Lacrosse case that would suggest that Crystal was just barely a person. The contempt and outright hatred for this woman proffered was that she had gone out on purpose to bring down innocent men in some kind of conspiracy with the Mike Nifong. Astonishing! It appeared as though the right-winged, disturbed individuals against Crystal had somehow gained access to the case file and could recite details that no one could know. That was, unless they had been granted access by the defense or the families of some of the lacrosse players. It seemed as though all of the energy, daily blog entries, and television coverage were parts of a planned negative public relations campaign.

Not once did those who sought to find faults in Crystal say anything at all about the party hosts. My conversations with Crystal and reporting by other sources suggested the players were a group of young men who were somewhat less ethical than Boy Scouts. At the party on 610 North Buchanan they said some very nasty things and their behavior was not stellar.

In the quest to find the truth, Crystal's judges took a side, but it still did not make sense that they were so concerned about this one woman. When I left my meetings with Crystal, I was more perplexed than ever as I read the descriptions of her in the opinion columns and blogs. Just how did they assume they could know enough about Crystal having never heard her speak? Why not just wait for the legal process to run its course?

The truth lies well beyond the headlines and opinion columns. Many people have failed to see a case that has multiple layers. The clearest one of the layers is race. The deeper I dug into the writings of Crystal's most ardent critics, one thought constantly emerged. These critics believed that white men in America were the ones who had suffered from discrimination. Their real motive appears to be maintaining the banner of angry white men. They are the people who trade on race, whether for their benefit or to cast aspersions; they take advantage of situations presented in this case. Then, whenever anyone wants to discuss the merits of the case, no one can really remember any of the facts. We are reduced to repeating propaganda and innuendo that was spread by the winning side.

As I talked with Crystal about the hours leading up to her arriving at the party, I could not get over how different I had pictured her. I assumed she had just come off a street corner somewhere in Durham. Based on what I had read, I never could have imagined her being an ordinary adult college student who had a family, friends, and a desire to work with troubled kids.

She had one brush with the law. While serious, it had been resolved and was not exactly as people painted it. By all accounts, Mangum was a good mother and involved with her children.

It was reasonable to make the ones who planned the party subject to some scrutiny if it was okay to dissect the accuser's life. Why do they get a complete pass when it comes to the significant issue of credibility? It is also curious that some argued that the partygoers' past criminal indiscretions were not a factor at all.

There has been a concerted effort from day one to muddy the waters about the case. While Mike Nifong did little to serve his cause by speaking publicly, it is not unusual for district attorneys to speak about cases. What is unusual here is how quickly and forcefully the weight of the national media, well-connected relatives, and high-priced lawyers came down on the accuser in the case.

It is true that Mike Nifong would have appeared to suffer the most fallout from the case; however, Crystal Mangum got pilloried as well. Her medical history, address, children's school, and false information about her person quickly and dramatically appeared on the Internet. Some of that information eventually worked its way to mainstream media outlets. It became a part of a narrative that suggested she was a prostitute, drug addict, and ne'er-do-well. It would not help that Jesse Jackson and Al Sharpton would wedge themselves into the middle of the case and not attempt to correct some of the bogus information being released about Crystal.

What emerges some two years later is that we can now see that the people who turned this case into a national spectacle were not the ones who wanted justice to prevail. The people who peddled the libelous and slanderous stories about Crystal are the same people who have been behind the Terri Shiavo case and worked on such causes as the Linda Tripp defense fund. Read the continual stream of columns, blogs, and opinion pieces about the Duke case and several names appear time and time again. I hate to encourage more reading of this stuff, but I must so that you can see for yourself. Look at some of the trash that has been written or appeared on television in the guise of legitimate journalism.

While the attorneys have been cautioned not to make public statements while there is still civil litigation, there is nothing to stop the so-called conservative commentators from speaking on behalf of the plaintiffs in the civil suits. Those same people who claim only to want justice were very good at turning the tide of public opinion in the original case. They were so good in fact, the pressure convinced North Carolina Attorney General Roy Cooper and the North Carolina Bar to take action against a sitting district attorney— something that had never been done in history.

I am suggesting that the Duke Lacrosse case narrative that you know and have come to believe is a lie. Going forward, expect to see an increase in the rhetoric coming from the flamethrowers on the political and religious right. There is still public opinion to influence.

I have recorded over 20 hours of interviews concerning Crystal's life and the events of March 13, 2006. The amount of time I've spent with Crystal is something I do not believe the police, Mike Nifong, or special prosecutors for the attorney general of North Carolina have done.

The most surprising thing of all is that when Crystal decided to write a book about her life, she was so open and talked candidly about her depression and past abuse. The journey over the past year as we completed this project has been very tough. We both have been disappointed at some of the responses that we have gotten when trying to get this story out. We've been lied to, threatened, and ignored. Despite all of that, this story is more important than many people realize. There are overwhelmingly complicated issues that need to be discussed. This book alone cannot address them all but it attempts to set a foundation on which they can be discussed rationally.

The insight gained while working with Crystal is something I could have never imagined while reading that first story sitting on that hard plastic chair at Midway Airport. Little did I know that all of the anguish I had experienced from reading the negative coverage about Crystal would become so challenging? This is the quintessential story about unfairness.

The portrait of Crystal Mangum as some delusional, drug-addled stripper is far from what I have experienced. I can say without equivocation that Crystal is not a drug abuser. She has maintained to me that the abuse of illegal or prescribed drugs has never been one of her problems, and I believe her.

While writing this book, I have had to assist Crystal explore serious issues about the choices she has made in her life. This project has forced Crystal to be bold and honest as she reveals her faults, personal tragedies, and just plain bad decisions that led her to 610 North Buchanan Boulevard that night in March 2006.

There is no way after reading this that you can view this case in the same way. You may still not believe that the three young men accused of rape should have been charged. We do not argue that. However, you will not believe all of the negative things you have heard about Crystal.

Because this case ended up being argued by the cable television "talking heads" you should not have expected the truth to emerge. I was amazed—you should be as well—at how so many people spoke with certainty about why the lacrosse players were innocent based on what they assumed was true about Crystal. However, what is the truth? Little, if anything, you heard about Crystal was based on any firsthand knowledge.

Family members, lawyers, and representatives of organizations who said they spoke on Crystal's behalf could not because they were not authorized to speak for her and most had never even met her. People who sat in judgment of Crystal because they read a police report on the North Carolina Department of Corrections Web site assumed they know everything they needed to know.

It is clear to me that her story deserves to be told. She has never been afforded a safe opportunity to speak for herself, and she wanted a chance to set the record straight. Despite her desire to speak out, Crystal has managed to stay out of the spotlight for almost two years. Some will probably criticize her for hiding from the media, but if you were in the same position, could you stand up to the scrutiny and attacks?

Crystal made it clear to me that the main reason she stayed out of the media glare is because she did not want every word she said to be evaluated and dissected. It would have been especially difficult when she did not have people around her who would be working in her best interest. Crystal really believed she would have her day in court. However, since we now know for absolutely certain that there will never be a trial for those accused of assaulting her, the only choice available is for her to tell her story.

Crystal feels she has been the one on trial. This ordeal has left her a troubled soul, with a tremendous amount of hurt and torment. If the Duke lacrosse players feel their life has been ruined, it goes without saying that Crystal feels the same way and worse. The players and their lawyers have been paid millions and still seek more.

It is with a great deal of pride that I say that I worked with Crystal to put her story on paper. I am proud because I know that the account of her life transcends the night of the party. Her life is a lesson for young girls and young men about the choices they make. It is about how to discern whom means you well and what is in your best interest. It is about how to live through the fire of such an intense amount of scrutiny and still emerge as a whole person.

This project is about helping Crystal repair her damaged life and preparing her to live for the rest of it in the service of others. Her story will also help you as it has gradually helped me put things into perspective. My life and yours are golden in comparison to millions of others who live with depression and have been burdened by years of physical, sexual, and emotional abuse. Now she lives with the added weight of always being connected to the Duke Lacrosse case.

I keep thinking about the lacrosse players hosting a party like the one that started this whole thing in the first place. Alcohol and scantily clad women do not make for a good mix if the men in the room cannot hold their liquor and are sexually misguided. What happened in the aftermath of the party should have caused people to consider the significant issues the story raises. Nevertheless, I know that it has not stopped more parties like the one held at 610 North

Buchanan Boulevard from happening nightly somewhere in America. Young men do not have to sexually exploit women and drink themselves into oblivion to have a good time and bond with each other. Sadly, the way our culture views it, if you do not do all those things you are not having a male experience.

What does it say about our society that a person feels no shame to bare their bodies for perfect strangers? It seems like there is almost an epidemic among college-aged women to bare themselves for things like *Girls Gone Wild*. What must be missing from a person's judgment center to make it seem reasonable to take off your clothes for very little or no money? To accept catcalls and to be groped by strangers must leave a stain on your psyche. I know women have been entertaining men with sex for centuries. Knowing about Crystal will not bring the practice to a halt. Crystal's story should at least cause some young women to consider what they let men do to them in the name of love or entertainment.

I ponder what would have happened if no protesters stood on the lawn at 610 North Buchanan banging pots. What if women's groups, black separatists, bloggers, satellite trucks, and high-priced lawyers stayed home and let the court settle this? I'd like to believe justice would still have been served.

Most of all I wonder about Mike Nifong and the way the case was handled. Surely, he must have had some evidence as he pushed forward. How else could he have brought such a case as far as he did if there was no evidence at all as the attorney general's report suggests. If it was to enable Mike Nifong to win the office of district attorney of Durham County, then he is indeed a very shallow man. The truth is he never needed a case like this to be elected. We could easily find hundreds of other cases handled by the prosecutors who serve the 100 counties in North Carolina where bias and withholding evidence led to convictions. Yet, in this state's entire history there has never been a district attorney dismissed from office for misconduct.

I believe the story of the Duke Lacrosse case is about a lot of things but none of them are what we have been told until now. The attorneys for the three accused did what they needed to do to insure their clients did not go to a trial. The strategy was to find the weak link for the prosecution. Unfortunately, it turned out that the weak link was the accuser's life story and not the facts of the case. Many crucial mistakes were made during the investigation that left the accuser, police, and district attorney on the defense. The reasons, I believe, the state of North Carolina intervened in this case were all political and had very little to do with wanting to find the truth. If finding the truth was the desired outcome, then we still do not have it.

If people were willing to tell the truth they would acknowledge that people produced to discredit Crystal were facing their own legal troubles and were represented by lawyers who were members of the players' defense team. They would come forward and tell why Crystal's medical records were leaked to the public to imply she had mental health problems. Others will say how they floated stories implying Crystal had been sexually promiscuous immediately before the alleged events when there was no proof she had been. Perhaps there is one person who will admit they were influenced to turn against Crystal for their own gain.

This is not an episode of "CSI" where everything is resolved in an hour. The intent of this book is not to prove that those who had been previously indicted did anything. What you will know at the end of this book is that Crystal Mangum is a human being above all else. She is not evil, a drug abuser, or a criminal. She has had a difficult life. Circumstances brought her to that place and time where things went terribly wrong. There was never any plan to hurt anyone or to cause any suffering. Now you will finally know Crystal Gail Mangum.

You will hear Crystal's story from her because she is capable of expressing what she wants to say. Throughout you will hear from both of us but mostly from Crystal. The way she talks about her life is dramatic and compelling. You will be moved to rethink what you have heard about her and the case.

During the past two years, many people associated with Crystal have been threatened and harassed. So, for their safety, some of the names have been changed when mentioning certain people and events in Crystal's life that do not have anything to do with the Duke Lacrosse case.

This is this first and best opportunity to hear Crystal's voice, and you should take the opportunity to listen.

March 2006

Deep down inside I should have known there was no getting ahead. It didn't take too long to figure out that the more you made the more you needed to make. That's why I had agreed to meet the lady from the escort service in the lobby of Burger King in the first place. She had seen me dancing at the Platinum Pleasures Club in Hillsborough. When she approached me, she told me I could make a lot more money doing private engagements. I did strongly think twice about not meeting her, but I rationalized it as a way to reach my goals quicker. It would be much more money than I could ever earn up on stage, and I didn't like the atmosphere in the clubs that much anyway. The one thing she pointed out about me was that I did not have a pimp like the other girls at the club. I wasn't a prostitute and wouldn't have all of what that meant hanging over me.

I'll leave my detailed views on the club for later. I will just say it wasn't the best place to work, and I didn't have a lot of friends there. For now what you need to know is that I was a freelancer, and I would not have to split the money with anyone else but the agency. They would find me gigs, and I could perform for people in their hotel rooms or at a private party. It was up to me what I was comfortable doing. The escort service did not arrange for sex with the clients so if a dancer chose to make her own side deals she would be the one who was taking all of the risk that came with that side deal. Since I was going into this strictly as a performer, sex with complete strangers was not something I was ever willing to consider. I told myself that I could stay away from that kind of thing although I knew that was the way many females supplemented their incomes.

The recruiter was telling me the inside scoop on the game, but it was not the one I intended to play. I could never see myself selling my body in that way. It was bad enough that I was dancing like this; I was not going to cross that line because there were too many other problems that came with it.

My family was at home and they were first and foremost in my life, no matter what else I was doing. I was doing this to take some of the burden off my boyfriend Mat. Things had been tough for us for a long time and this was one way to insure that I made it through college and the kids had a decent life. My goal was to get a master's degree or a PhD.

I know it is really hard for people to believe that after all that has been said about me that I was not a call girl. The truth is I chose to escort with a lot of hesitation. I knew what could happen and my conscience still weighed heavily on me about dancing in the first place. The money, getting into drugs, or drinking too much alcohol could easily set a person on the path to selling her body. I had been through more sexual abuse than you could ever imagine so this was not something I took lightly. I knew that I was carrying baggage from my early sexual experiences, and it permeated my entire life. There wasn't a day that went by that I didn't have to fight the depression that was the result of things that had happened to me long ago. It was also clear from talking to the other girls in the business that almost every one of them had been or were still being sexually abused. I was on a very slippery slope, and I had to keep my guard up if I was going to pull off this escort business.

I also had to make sure I could keep my personal and business relationships separate. I had to still be a mother, student, and partner. I had made several mistakes early on when I started dancing by becoming too friendly with people for whom I danced. Sometimes people did not understand that I was an entertainer. My job was to make them feel like they were special and the only one for that moment. That was it. All I could or was willing to do was strictly to entertain in the club or wherever I danced. Because I had been too friendly when I first started, several men tried to contact me away from the club when I made the fatal error of giving out my real name and phone number. I couldn't risk bringing that kind of thing to my house anymore. I was never going to do that again. I believed the escort service might provide me an added shield between my personal and professional life.

Believe it or not, there is substantial business *not* having sex with clients. People have all kinds of sexual desires and fantasies. I was willing to accommodate a very narrow range of fantasy. You do what you are comfortable with doing. One of the activities I was comfortable doing was performing in front of a couple. I would dance suggestively and sometime masturbate with sex toys while the couple had sex on the bed beside me. They did not touch me and I did not touch them. That's just the way it went. It isn't easy to admit that was what I was doing, but it is the truth. I don't suppose most people would consider what I was doing right or a moral thing to do, but I did it. People like the ones who paid for the service are probably working beside you right now. I'm not trying to suggest that everyone engages escorts but many people do and you would be surprised who they are. The same applies to the people who frequented the club looking to be entertained.

It is incredibly difficult to describe what it felt like, doing what I did in front of perfect strangers. What I can tell you is that you almost have to leave your body. Detach completely and go to another place all together. Alcohol ably assisted me in making the break from reality. I had to drink before doing the escort jobs and while at the club, so I would not think about the kids or my boyfriend. It was painful even though the bills were being paid. I had problems with alcohol in the past, and it was very dangerous mixing it with the business I was engaged in. Nevertheless, there is a fine line: I could not drink too much or I would lose control. That's when things could go very wrong, and I could not afford for that to happen. I believed I knew what my limit was.

For sure there were plenty of other women at the club or working for the escort services who were willing to do whatever to make the extra money. I still had a boyfriend at home who I loved very much. We had a normal sex life, and it was enjoyable as much as it could be. Even though we had been together for about six years in 2006, I still found it difficult to allow myself to be completely sexually satisfied with him. My boyfriend, on the other hand, was well taken care of and he pleased me as much as I allowed him. So, as I danced in the club and for these private parties, I could not see myself betraying him by having sex with a total stranger for money. What I was doing was bad enough. I know for sure he did not like me dancing one bit, but he set boundaries, and I honored them. I could do what I was doing as long I came home before 2:00 am, and I didn't do anything to put our relationship in more jeopardy than I had already. I just had to keep telling myself that this was not going to last forever—that there was a good reason for doing this. I would not have any student loans, the kids could go places and have things I didn't have while I was growing up. I would eventually just melt right back into the real world as soon as I graduated from college.

In retrospect I can with all honesty say that this was a bad way to make a living. I denied it even as I saw girls at the club do things that they knew were not good for them. The drugs, the complete and total control of their lives by pimps, and the utter dysfunction was stark. All the girls probably said to themselves at one point that this was just for the bills but the truth is they were never getting far enough ahead no matter how much they believed they were in control. There is much more I want to say about this, and I will later, but it is important to know right now how I felt about exotic dancing as I was about to tempt fate one too many times. It takes something drastic to happen to get you out of the dancing and the escort businesses. I was in too deep and was not going to get out on my own. I was starting to engage in dangerous behavior but the consequences had not been bad enough to catch up with me yet. My bills were paid and my worries seemed small in comparison to the other folks around me. I forgot all about morals and God. I had to harden my heart and turn a blind eye to the evil upon which this industry is built. The wake up call was about to come. March 13, 2006 was going to end my dancing career.

So the meeting in Burger King convinced me that I could handle this type of work if I just kept to what I said I was going to do. Just remember, it was only a way to supplement the club work, which could be slow at times. The owner of the particular escort service who called me for the assignment that would forever link me with the Duke Lacrosse case was a lady named Tammy. I felt she had looked out for me by picking me out at the club, and she seemed so willing to teach me the ropes of the business. She let me in on the tricks of trade and how to get every penny out of the customer while staying within the bounds I had set for myself. She was street-smart and knew how to get a person who wasn't interested to go along with just about anything. Additionally, she knew my boundaries and had set me up with the kind of jobs she knew I was comfortable handling. The first three assignments with the agency were as uneventful as these things could be. No problems so far.

March 13, 2006, started out unspectacularly. Sometime around 10:00 am I decided to start working on my hair and nails. I was not sure I would get a call, but I went about my business hoping I would hear from the escort service. They told me that getting work would not be a difficult proposition, and I could stay pretty busy. I had already done a few jobs during the past days and the prospect of having a little more money had me ready to go. My friend Jerriel Johnson had driven me to the other recent gigs. They were uneventful. I was not an expert and had not been doing this for very long so it all appeared straightforward and very doable.

Tammy called me around noon to let me know she had an opportunity for me to make some decent money. The first three engagements I had done for her agency had all been for couples, and I didn't expect anything else. I was at my parents' house when I got the call. Tammy could not tell me exactly what the details were at the time but said she would get back with me in the afternoon. She mainly wanted to know if I was available, and I said I would be.

I got the second call from Tammy around 3:30 pm to confirm I was still available and to give me the added details about the engagement. This time she told me it was going to be a bachelor party. The future groom was a guy named Dan Flanagan who called to make the arrangements. I was to later learn that was not his real name, and that he had specifically requested girls that were not black to entertain. Consequently, it was not going to be the typical hotel thing I did with couples. She was clear that this was going to be a bachelor party for a few guys, and it paid $800. Moreover, in this conversation she told me there would be a second dancer there to meet me. That meant the $800 was suddenly $400. Actually, it would be even less after I gave the escort service their cut and paid someone to drive me there. At best I could end up with about $175 if I didn't get any tips. Despite that, it still seemed an okay deal, and I committed to going. Tammy further explained it would be about five or six guys there and last about two hours from 11:00 to 1:00. She asked me if I could handle that and I said yes. I didn't think a group of five would be so different than two. Had it been more than five I believe I would have turned it down. Nevertheless, I had danced at the club in front of far more people than that. I thought what could happen if I was just going to dance? I told her it would be no problem for me, and I agreed to take the assignment. We were to talk later if anything changed.

I immediately called my friend Jerriel who had driven me to other engagements, but I was unable to get a hold of him. I went ahead and made plans to go anyway. Before I continue here, I know there has been some discussion and eyebrows raised about having people drive me to my gigs. Having a driver is part of the business for a vast majority of the girls. Not only does the driver make sure you get where you need to go but also serves as protection. No matter how good a person a client seems to be, an escort service cannot guarantee your safety. You have to be protected as much as you can, but it isn't always sufficient. A driver provides a level of comfort that allows you to go about your business and get back home safely. Besides, Jerriel was a friend and a fellow student at North Carolina Central University. I trusted him and he wanted to make sure I was going to be okay if I was going to do this kind of thing. Jerriel also knew my boyfriend and that made it more comfortable for Mat to know that I was being watched after.

I figured I could find a ride eventually and did not sweat it at first because there was still plenty of time to find someone to take me. Plus, the party was right here in Durham and could not be that far from where I was living at the time. Unfortunately, Jerriel did call me back later with disappointing news. He said he could not take me. He had other plans and there was no way he could swing it. I believe deep inside he was concerned for my safety, but he would never say it. Jerriel is a good guy and—just like I was—

working his way through college. Assisting me would make going to college a little easier for Jerriel or anyone who could drive me around. Having a little more money in his pocket would not be a bad thing, but he told me I would have to find someone else to take me. I had no reason to believe that going to this appointment would be any less safe than any others I had done in the past. As I look back now, perhaps I should not have been so nonchalant but there was no hint I needed to take any extra precaution.

I was going to have to make alternate plans to get to the party. At one point I even thought about asking my dad to take me. However, there seemed to be something a bit creepy about that and not right so I let that idea fade quickly. My father knew I had been doing exotic dancing, but I could not bring myself to ask him to be my driver. I didn't want to seem that desperate and decided to try and reach my friend Brian who knew I was a dancer and who would probably help me out. We had known each other for some time, and he had graciously helped me get to work in Hillsborough. He was a student at North Carolina Central and like me a psychology major. We had similar ambitions to become counselors and help kids in trouble. It turned out that he was available. I trusted him and had known he would be reliable. I had been redoing my nails in anticipation of the party, and finished up at my father's house. I did ask my father to take me to Brian's house. I was dropped off there about 9:45 pm, where I took a shower and waited for the escort service to call with directions.

That call came at 10:00 pm. It was Melissa, my other contact with the service. She described the same kind of bachelor party that Tammy had earlier. She told me to go to 610 North Buchanan Boulevard to meet with the future groom, Dan Flanagan. The other dancer would be responsible for getting there on her own. At that time I still had no idea who she might be. Even at this point, neither Melissa nor Tammy mentioned that the man hiring the dancers was not expecting black women or hinted that the size of the gathering was going to be anything beyond six people. Two substantial lies had been told. If the escort service knew the request was for white women, they should have obliged their customer and never sent either one of us on the assignment. It was also extremely troubling that the person who called to make the arrangements initially lied and purposely underrepresented how many people were going to be at the event. I would imagine only a few dancers would have wanted to perform for the kind of money being offered for such a large crowd.

Now with the address we left Brian's house at a little after 10:30 pm, but we had trouble finding the place. We drove around for some time, and I started to worry that I might get there late. Frustrated and not exactly sure where 610 North Buchanan was, I called my dad for better directions. He pointed us right to where we needed to go. We arrived at the house at about 11:15 pm. One of the big ironies is that the house is located only blocks from where I attend church. It is just a brisk walk away from where I have been going to seek some spiritual comfort.

As soon as we pulled in front of the house, I got an uneasy feeling. I could clearly see that there were at least 20 guys milling around in the backyard. This was not the bachelor party that Tammy and Melissa had described to me twice that day. It looked more like frat house with a bunch of teenagers out to have a good time at all costs. *This couldn't be where I was supposed to be!*

I hesitated at first but then told Brian I would be okay and got out of the car. I headed directly for the backyard where I saw the people gathered. There I saw a woman standing with several white males who looked very young. She had to be the second dancer because she was the only other woman there besides me. This would be the first and only time I would formally meet the woman who I would later find out was Kim Roberts, aka Kim Pittman. She said her name was Nikki and we hugged in a friendly embrace. I introduced myself using my staged name, "Precious." There was no need for her to know my real name. That's how the business goes. I might never see her again, and I still needed to keep a wall between my business and personal life. We did make a little small talk. Nikki told me she had a son and was doing the best she could to support him. I genuinely thought about my two kids as she was talking. It's a tough way to make a living, and I admired her in the way only another dancer could understand. Not for doing the work but for trying to take care of her business without the help of the system or being dependent on a man that meant you no good.

"Have you ever performed for a big crowd like this before?" Nikki asked.

I admitted that I hadn't performed in this kind of setting. I had performed for a bigger number of people in the club but everything in the club is controlled, there are bouncers, and people clearly know the rules. There you danced on stage to try and entice guys to pay extra money for you to entertain them in the VIP room. Not everyone paid attention to you because there were other things going on around you. Besides, there were many more girls who would come out to perform. The bouncers are never more than an arm's-length away and can keep even the most obnoxious people under control. The escort stuff was one or two persons and the driver was always nearby so I didn't have many worries about that kind of work either. This, on the other hand, was much different than anything I had ever done before. I genuinely thought it was the only right thing to do to admit to Nikki that I was inexperienced entertaining in this kind of setting.

We chatted for a minute or two longer. I guess she figured we'd better have a plan or things might not go well. *This was going to be interesting.*

"Come on, let's go inside and get our routine together," Nikki said.

The person I believed was Dan Flanagan met with us. He gave me $400 in twenty dollar bills, and I put the money in my makeup bag. He handed Nikki the rest of the money. I imagine it was also $400 dollars, but I have no way to be certain about that. We walked together up the back stairs leading into the house. Dan politely opened the door and let us in. He took us to the bathroom where we could get ready and Nikki could change. I came already prepared to dance, but I still needed to check myself in the mirror, get my makeup together, and calm my nerves before I went onto the dance floor. We closed the door behind us.

Minutes later, there was a knock on the bathroom door. It was Dan again. This time he had drinks for us. I had two Ice House beers while I was at Brian's house. As I said before, drinking was a part of my preparation for performing. I had to be at least a little tipsy to be mellowed out enough to perform. As they say, alcohol can give you liquid courage. Without it I know I would likely not have ever been able to perform. But you can't be drunk.

The one thing I never did or would do—illegal drugs. This night, I did not take any prescription or over-the-counter drugs either. It would come as a shock to me when I learned that there were reports that I was on a strong cocktail of drugs to treat bipolar disorder the night of March 13. The surprise for me was that there was no evidence of that. That was one of the rumors used to discredit me. I was completely aware of the dangers of taking the medications I had been prescribed with alcohol. It would have been dangerous not only on account of the side effects but also because I needed to have some sense of where I was for my own safety. I did have prescriptions for a number of drugs at home. I have no problem admitting taking those drugs in the past. There was just no proof I had taken them that night. There are also no toxicology reports from that night, either. To the best of my knowledge, no such test was performed when I went to the hospital. Even so, if a toxicology test had been performed it would have only shown I had alcohol from the beer I drank and the traces from whatever was in the drink I received when I was in the bathroom. Performing a toxicology test is one of the things I wish had been done as part of the investigation.

I believe information about the drugs for which I had valid prescriptions had to have come from my medical records or the doctors who had been treating me. Every thinking person should be outraged that this was allowed to happen. There was no reason for that information to become public at the time other than to suggest that I was to blame for what I had reported. Who released my records? Would the others who were involved in the case been okay with releasing their records? I suspect they would have cried foul play if the district attorney had moved to collect medical information about them. Shortly after the incident gained national exposure, the doctor who I believe may have revealed some of my medical history told me he could no longer treat me because he had a conflict of interest. The doctor said he had connections to Duke and maintained it would be inappropriate to continue treating me, and that I should see someone else. I will have more to say about my mental health status as my story progresses.

It is true that a lot of girls in the business use crack, methamphetamines, prescription drugs, or whatever else they are addicted to as a way of getting them through these horrible ordeals. Especially for those who get into the business because they are addicted already, the need for more and more drugs leaves them exposed to all kinds of abuse and mistreatment. There is a very thin line between numbing yourself and becoming dependent on drugs to be able to cope with life day-to-day. I could not have performed if I was so adversely affected by too many drugs. On this night in particular, I drank less than I would normally. Because there would be more than two people, I needed to have my wits about me. I did feel the need for alcohol on any ordinary night so it would be a lie to say that I didn't have anything. I would say I certainly needed it that night to calm my nerves and give myself the liquid courage to go before such a large crowd.

We will never be sure what was in the drinks that Dan gave us. I do not know who made them or what they contained. I just remember taking a few sips and sitting the glass on the edge of the sink. Later as we maneuvered around the tiny bathroom, I accidentally spilled the rest of the drink into the sink. Nikki then offered me some of her drink, but I declined.

The assembled crowd was obviously getting impatient as various people kept coming to the door trying to get us to hurry up and come out. Eventually, the tone became even more heated as there was screaming for us to hurry up, and demands to "see some action" started to come from the other room. Then I heard it for the first time; someone in the crowd was referring to us as "black bitches." It was not said just once. It was almost as if that was our names. I didn't want to come out of the bathroom at that point. For that matter, what right did they have in calling me bitch or any name? I was hired to dance for a bachelor party and obviously that wasn't where I found myself. Someone had lied and now I was being demeaned for no reason. This kind of dancing isn't the most respectable business to most people, but they had crossed the line already, and I had not even hit the dance floor.

Nikki and I talked about things. We were going to go out anyway and perform. Nothing elaborate, I would work on one side of the room and she on the other. I was going to take my chances that nothing would happen. Brian knew where I was and so did the escort service. Just ignore the name calling, and I could get through this. I was already here and I had their money. We walked out of the bathroom together and into the living room. There were at least 30 or more people standing around. I thought to myself "five?" There were way more than five and this wasn't a bachelor party.

The music was already playing when we entered the room. I started to dance just like I had planned to and so far there was nothing unusual. As I moved around, I could see Nikki out of the corner of my eye. It seemed as though less than five minutes had passed. Nikki was well into her routine already. Her body jerking in time to the music, I couldn't believe what I was seeing. I thought to myself, "Is she naked?" She was! We had only been performing a matter of minutes and Nikki had taken things way beyond anything I had planned. I glanced and saw her panties lying beside her. I could clearly see her pubic region.

I knew some girls did not mind being completely nude, but I did. One girl can set the stage for the type of interaction the people at a strip party expect. If the first girl takes off her clothes then all of the girls are expected to follow. That also goes for performing sex acts, either real or simulated ones. If the crowd gets the impression that anything goes, then *anything* goes. Obviously, the clothes I was wearing didn't leave much to the imagination but it is a different proposition than being completely naked. Nudity suggests that you are willing to go to other places that I wasn't about to go to. Sure, you could probably make more money, but it wasn't worth the risk in a crowd like this. They didn't seem all that savvy on strip culture and didn't look as though they were willing to part with more money for a little extra skin to show. I was content with dancing and being suggestive. Obviously, I had been naked in front of complete strangers before. I could not do the part of the couples' work where I masturbated if I had my clothes on. So, let me make it clear that I'm not saying that I had never performed while naked. It just wasn't a good idea for Nikki to do it in this setting and besides she had not discussed that aspect with me. The image of her partially naked caught me off guard. I lost my balance. All of a sudden, I felt dizzy and stumbled and in a flash I landed awkwardly, almost on top of Nikki.

I know that some accounts have suggested that this episode meant that Nikki and I had planned some routine that involved us simulating girl-on-girl sex but that is so far from the truth. Perhaps the boys believed that all performances like this ended up with a lesbian sex act. Maybe they had been watching too many porn movies or wanted that to happen. I'm sure they could have specified that as a request to the escort service when they called to make arrangements, but I had no idea that there was any suggestion at all that anyone would be removing their clothes let alone be engaging in a lesbian sex act in front of a room filled with loutish men in their late teens and early twenties. The way I ended up on the floor was completely an accident and the result of my complete and utter surprise at what was going on. The people who have suggested otherwise do not have any basis for their claim. No one could have interpreted what had just happened as a planned routine. My one and only thought about the entire situation was, "What the hell was Nikki doing?"

Completely disoriented at that point I just wanted to get up and get out of there. In a flash Nikki moved to help me and scrambled to get her panties. I moved as quickly as I could to get to my feet. By now the crowd was in a frenzy. I'm sure they didn't know what to make of what they had just seen. Over the noise I positively believed I heard someone yell, "We are going to stick this broom up your asses!" I could see one of them as he waved a broomstick in our direction.

"We need to get out of here. They are going to try and use that broom on us," Nikki screamed at me over the chaos. She looked scared and I felt it.

By now I heard the words nigger, bitch, and other names. They were definitely not happy with the performance. It seemed as though the entire crowd was going to converge on us. They were so much more vocal than the people I danced for at the Platinum Club, and they looked as though they wanted to provoke a confrontation. I knew they were angry about how things were turning out, but I had to consider the reason I said I was doing this in the first place.

This was supposed to be a way I could better take care of my kids and put me in a better place in the future. Right now, I knew that this was out of control, and I needed to get out. We were not being respected and I did not feel safe. Even though I did the kind of work that I did, I still expected some level of respect. The money I was paid did not entitle anyone to threaten or mistreat me in any way. That was enough for me to call it quits. I left the living room and headed to the bathroom to get my things. That was going to be the end of the show for me. We hurriedly collected the things we had left in the bathroom and retreated outside with every intention of leaving, but we were followed by three of the partygoers. We quickly got in the car but did not have time to pull away.

A person I believe to be David Evans, one of the players subsequently indicted, was among the group that followed us to the car. My best recollection is he and the other two went to the driver's-side car window and spoke to Nikki, pleading for us to come back inside. I was fuming and wanted to go and would have right then had I been behind the wheel of the car. But the men standing at Nikki's window apologized for what happened and promised not to let things get out of hand. Evans added, "The guys, they listen to me," implying that somehow he could get them under control and get them to act like they had some sense. To that point I could say I didn't trust his assessment of his leadership ability. He had failed so far and needed to do something substantial to get me to go back inside. He said he might be able to get us more money if we returned and the guys would be angry if we just left.

I know there has been a lot made of the fact that we were there to "shakedown" these rich Duke kids for money. However, at this point I still had no idea who these people were. They certainly didn't appear to have a lot of money from the condition of the house. After all, they were trying to pay two people $800 to entertain a group of almost 40. I'm sure the reason for the initial lie about the bachelor party had to do with the fact that they didn't want to part with too much money in the first place. Their promising us more money to come back inside wasn't going to yield a lot more money, but I was about to net less than $200 for all the trouble I had been through.

We decided that we would go back in, but I was still feeling out of sorts and not myself. I can't really say what the exact feeling was. It wasn't like a high feeling from drinking. I knew what that felt like, and it was something more. I was still a little dizzy like I had been when I stumbled while dancing but not to the point where I thought I would collapse or pass out. I was aware of my surroundings and wanted to pay attention to everything that was going on around me. The best way to describe it is that I just felt out of place.

Looking back on it now, it would be easy to suggest all kinds of reasons for the way I was feeling. I was probably more scared than anything else. It was a very heated situation and when we returned to the house through the kitchen, things had not calmed down. The atmosphere was still charged, and I felt like things were escalating. As soon as we reentered the house we were confronted by a group of angry guys. It seemed as though they were yelling and screaming at the tops of their lungs. I felt even more in a panic when I saw one of the guys go to the door we had just entered, to close and lock it behind us. That struck me as odd since people had been moving freely in and out all night. That move seemed especially sinister in light of the way everyone was acting.

I would suppose that at this point there had been enough of a commotion to call some attention to what was going on at the house. The crowd was extremely agitated. I can't imagine that neighbors weren't getting fed up with all of the noise that was coming from the house. Perhaps locking the door was to keep anyone for coming in and out and draw less attention to the mess of a party that was going on. However, it did cross my mind that it could also be because they planned to make us pay for leaving the house in the first place and not giving them the kind of show they had expected. My gut told me we were in for real trouble. Almost immediately and amid the chaos, I became separated from the woman I knew as Nikki. There seemed to be guys everywhere, and I couldn't tell where she had gone. The people there were much bigger and taller than I was. When I lost sight of Nikki, I felt completely surrounded. We had barely known each other for 30 minutes, and now I was frantically looking for her so that we could escape. Everything was happening so quickly; I was just trying to keep myself together.

A lot of people seem to positively assume we were at the house all night, and that I should remember every detail about the carpet, furniture, and who was standing exactly where. Before this incident, I was not the best person at remembering minute details about my surroundings. I am poor with directions and under the best circumstance I will still need to call for directions even in my hometown. Even if I can't remember the smallest detail, I do know what happened to me in that house after I became separated from Nikki. People can argue forever whether the men ultimately charged with assaulting me were the right people, but I will never say that nothing at all happened that night.

The crush of people and unfamiliar surroundings make it that much harder to make a positive identification of who assaulted me. I depended on the police investigators and hoped that one of the people at the party would be willing to come forward and tell the truth about what went on that night. Something did happen. Something that would change my life and the lives of countless others, for as long as we all live.

Instead of going back in order to dance, I was forced into the bathroom with three of the partygoers. I was grabbed by the throat and quickly subdued. There were two people in front of me and one in the back. I tried to pull away but one of them grabbed my arm and pulled me back. The one holding my arm said, "Sweetheart, you can't leave." He then stood behind me while another stood in the front. I could hear yelling in the other room. It sounded like the way people scream and cheer at a football game. I screamed, too, hoping someone would hear me but no one came to my rescue.

Family

I believe it is only fair that I be allowed to tell you something about my family and myself. When my name was released in the media it was often mispronounced as Crystal Gail Mangrum. It is Mangum! I am proud of who I am and where I was born. Durham, North Carolina, has been my home since July 16, 1978.

I am the youngest child of Travis and Mary Mangum, both of whom I consider to be loving and caring parents who raised me as well as they knew how. I grew up in an often chaotic but strict Christian home with my sister Marella and brother Travis, Jr., not far from the campuses of Duke and North Carolina Central universities. Those two schools are separated only by a few miles but might as well have been light years away in the minds of the hordes of reporters who descended on my hometown in the wake of the scandal. Everyone had some knowledge that Duke was a great place to get an education and high class. If people did not know what lacrosse was, they knew about the Blue Devil basketball team.

As a child I spent my early life at 2910 Cedarwood Drive in the very normal and middle class Forestview Heights neighborhood. Forestview was not a bad place for a kid to grow up in. Black folks who had decent jobs and families lived there and wanted the same things as everyone else. They kept their lawns cut and kids played under the watchful eyes of the mothers. All three of Travis and Mary's children have developed very distinct personalities despite having grown up in the same household. Our differences probably stem from the fact that there is an age gap between us. My brother Travis is 12 years older and Marella is three years older than I am.

My parents are good working-class folks who were trying to protect me, their baby. I feel as though the media used my parents. More than once they appeared on television looking totally out of their element. It was the proverbial "deer in the headlights" look. Every news organization was looking forward to talking to anyone in my family. This placed my parents in an awkward situation. They knew very little about the party on March 13 and what was going on with the police investigation. I didn't tell them because I didn't want to. It was difficult enough and I had already been through a lot in my life and this was another heart wrenching episode; I wanted to spare them. My parents and other family members appeared on television far too often and only insured that matters would be worse.

Therefore, I want people to know that during all the turmoil in my childhood and throughout my life, one thing remained constant for me and that is to say that my dad was my hero. I looked to my dad for answers because he always seemed to have a solution for everything. I had and still have great respect for him. My dad was never too macho to do the things one would expect only their mother to do. Sometimes he would work hard all day and then cook dinner for the family as soon as he returned home. So, I can't be too angry with him about all of the television interviews.

My dad was also the one to save my sister and me from a great deal of anguish when he taught our mother how to correctly fix our hair. Our mother would always start at the roots and pull hard. Dad on the other hand combed gently. He started at the ends and would gently comb our hair to the back like you were supposed too. It wasn't as though my mother didn't try—I cherish her—but my dad always took over because she often didn't meet our expectations or didn't know how to do certain things.

I can't recall most of my very early childhood but one memory stands out to me about the time I was eight-years-old. My father left home for work one morning and did not return for some time. It would be one of the several times when I lost a parent at a critical time in my life. At each point they would leave and return but never as the same person. It was both sad and frightening not to have my father around. When I finally got a chance to see him, I stared into his eyes and poured out all the emotion. I was a little girl who had missed her daddy. I wanted and needed for him to have one of his ready answers.

"Daddy," I inquired, "what's the matter with you?"

"My back hurts," he replied. The pain registered on his face. It wasn't just an ordinary backache.

"What happened? Is that why you can't work anymore?"

"I hurt my back at work and the doctors did the best they could, but I will never be the same person I used to be," he insisted with an earnest look in his face. He pulled up his shirt to reveal a huge scar from his rib cage down to his belly button.

I clung to every word as he described the accident. That was the moment when everything changed for the family for good. When things became hard for us and there was no steady and reliable income at times. It was also the first and last time I saw my dad cry. The only time he ever really looked as though he was in fear and had worries. He looked really vulnerable and it caused me to really worry too. For the first time, my superhero was just human and just my dad.

My father had always been a person with a strong work ethic. He worked as much as humanly possible to take care of his family of five. He would often work 10 extra hours a week in a restaurant in addition to holding two full time regular jobs. I can only hope to be as strong as my dad when it comes to the desire to care for and provide for the family.

On my dad's first job, he was a truck driver for a moving company. It was both physically and emotionally draining work for him. The job required him to lift heavy object in excess of 80 pounds all the while he was being berated and made to feel less than human by his white co-workers. It was on his second full time job where he would have a very serious accident that would profoundly affect the entire family until this very day.

Even though it was the beginning of his shift, my father was finding it hard to muster the energy for another eight-hour job. He had already put in the time at his first job, and he didn't feel as though he had the energy to make it through on account of all the other work, he had already done. My dad's second job was in construction, and it required that you have the energy to do work that was as challenging and strenuous as his first job. He was often required to transport materials from one job site to another. Because he was one of the youngest and strongest of the workers, he was always tapped to be the one who did the heavy work.

This particular day, the construction company was moving supplies and material on a freight train. My dad's job was to help load the cargo and make sure the load had not shifted or was damaged in transit. He had also found that he was spending a lot of his time watching for thieves who aimed to steal from the train when it made its stops.

As the freight train was loaded and the crew prepared to move on to its destination, my father felt himself in a state of complete exhaustion. Nevertheless, he still climbed aboard the side of the train and firmly gripped the pole that he would hold onto for the short ride to the first stop.

The hours of work had started to accumulate and the exhaustion was unbearable. My father strained to keep his heavy eyelids from closing completely. Just at that moment he could no longer hold his eyelids open, the train stopped suddenly. It was then that it was clear that working 18 hours a day was too much of a strain on his body. My father was affected in every way. His normal reaction time was compromised, and he could not think clearly. He just could no longer hold onto the handrail and he lost his grip. As soon as he released, out of control, my father flew into the grass embankment beside the railroad tracks.

My father was disoriented and in pain, but he did have the presence of mind to raise his hand to try and flag down the train. None of the people on the train noticed they had lost a crewmember or saw him waving and the train drove out of sight. He kept his hand raised, but he couldn't move the rest of his body. The jolt from the hard landing sent pain shooting through his entire body.

Even though the train had been long gone, my father kept his hand in the air. He could only hope that someone could see him from the road and come to his rescue. After lying there for several minutes he could feel the presence of someone standing over him. It was a very short woman with a large frame. The woman was in her late 50's. She had noticed him from the road that ran adjacent to the railroad tracks as she drove by.

The Good Samaritan already was slightly bent over, but she leaned closer and finally knelt down beside him. She spoke in a motherly voice and said, "Son, everything will be all right."

My dad told me how glad he was to see the woman. He had believed no one would find him there. He tried to reach out to her but the pain was excruciating, and she shouted back at him, "Don't move. I'm sure you're hurt badly. Don't worry, I will get help, and you are going to be okay!"

My father turned his head slightly away as she got up and disappeared out of sight back to the road. He hadn't said a word to her. He could only hope she was telling the truth, and she wouldn't leave him there.

Just as the lady promised, she did return. This time she was accompanied by the sound of sirens. At last he could relax. My father told me that he actually was so at ease that he drifted off to sleep after the paramedics loaded him into the ambulance. Both the lady and the paramedics were amazed at his ability to go to sleep at a time like this. Not knowing what was going on, they feared he was going into a coma and they went to work keeping him awake. Trying to keep my father awake was frustrating for the ambulance crew, and they became impatient and worn out. Little did they know that he was just plain exhausted. He had been working so hard that he was just not able to stay alert. This was the first time his body was able to rest.

The day of the accident marked the beginning of three long months in the Durham County Hospital for my father. He suffered cracked ribs, an injured spine, countless cuts and bruises all over his body and to his face. The doctors were amazed that he had managed to survive such a horrible accident.

My father told me about how he would lie in his hospital bed thinking about how much of a bind he had put his family in. In his effort to support his family, he had worked so hard to the point where he injured and almost killed himself. Now there was no one to take care of things. If only he had listened to his body and worked on one less job, the family would have still been poor but not as poor as we would be now without him being able to work. He thought about how hard it was going to be for my mother. He sank into a deep depression blaming himself for ruining the family.

We needed my father to break out of his depression. We just needed him to be able to help the family. Things got so tight for some time, I genuinely believe even the dog started to notice. It would be two or three days that went by before we would have dog food.

After several months of severe physical and emotional pain, we got a break. My father was unaware that he had been eligible for disability payments that would give the family some support. He was notified that he was entitled to an initial check of $40,000. That would be the start of his disability benefits as he was no longer able to work. In addition, the company he worked for offered him another $60,000 in workmen's compensation insurance. With the sum of the two settlements, the family was not only going to be able to recover, but we would thrive for a while.

It seemed as though my father was always sad about what happened to him. However, I know he was relieved that his family was being taken care of. There was food on the table, and he could buy things for us. The creditors who had been hounding him were off his back and for a change the relationship between him and my mother seemed to be good.

With the money from the settlement, my parents decided to fix up the house, add a garage, replace the vinyl siding and the windows. They even started adding new and expensive furniture to every room in the house. In addition, for the first time, my siblings and I were rewarded with an allowance so that we could purchase new clothes and shoes. My mom would suggest that we only purchase expensive name brand items with our newfound wealth.

The spending didn't stop with the house. Because the family's overall financial situation improved, so did their credit situation, and they decided to purchase a brand new car. Of course all of the spending would come to an end when my parents realized that the money had been used up. In two years the entire settlement was gone, and we found ourselves slowly sinking back into debt and poverty. The only income we had was our dad's monthly disability checks.

Desperate not to lose everything me father tried to convince the doctors he could work so he could regain his position at his former company. He assumed he could at least be a truck driver, but he was unable to pass the physical examinations.

Financially, the family was in a bind again and my father knew the disability check alone was not going to be enough so he decided to set up a shade-tree mechanics shop in his brand-new garage to help make ends meet. He became a well-known mechanic around our community. As I got older he would work on my classmates' cars and cars that belonged to their parents. Many times over the years he had talked about closing the garage on account of his physical limitations, but he couldn't because it kept our family together.

I believe the story about my father is important for many reasons. It is a sign of the kind of man he is and why he felt it was important to defend me. He had always gone the extra mile for all of us—trying to be a man and teaching us the difference between right and wrong. It also sometimes led him to make some bad decisions.

It was very difficult seeing my dad try to speak to the media and my mother trying to stop him. I can only imagine what people thought about both of my parents because of what they saw. It broke my heart because every time any one from the family appeared on television, I got angry. I didn't want to be angry, but it was painful to see.

Even more disturbing was when some of my other relatives started to appear on television. People like my brother and my cousin Jackie. Even though most of the time they talked positively about me, they never once talked to me about the case. At the time I wasn't talking to my brother at all.

As for my cousin, we had not seen each other in years but had talked on the phone. With the passing of time, I have confirmed what I suspected, that Jackie had been out trying to sell my life story. I have learned from several major media sources that my own cousin asked for money on my behalf. Apparently, making the rounds in New York with someone I didn't know, Jackie left a lasting negative impression about me.

I discovered Jackie's escapades when I was trying to get major media outlets to let me tell my story. For example, I found out from CNN that Jackie had arranged for me to comment on the attorney general's dismissal of the charge on the day it happened. Unbeknownst to me, CNN had rented a ballroom in a hotel in downtown Durham to host our entire family and get reactions. Needless to say, I didn't show for that because I had no idea that the event was taking place.

One other thing about cousin Jackie is that she is really a "he." Jackie was born Clyde. That fact alone doesn't mean anything other than he believes he should have been a "she." The more serious problem is the lies and deceit that my cousin pulled on people in my name. I imagine someone paid some money for my cousin to talk. For the media who did pay, shame on them. For the media that didn't pay, they still should be ashamed and should have known better then to put Jackie or anyone except me in front of the camera.

As for reconciling with my family—that will happen at some point. I talk to my parents because I love them. I also know they were manipulated by people like Durham attorney Mark Simeon who claimed to represent me. Not only had I never talked to Mr. Simeon, he was also supposed to be representing Kim Roberts, the other dancer, as well. Talk about a conflict. Especially because Mr. Simeon was with Ms. Roberts when she gave her famous "60 Minutes" interview with Ed Bradley.

I don't know how I would have handled the reporters coming to knock at my door at all hours if I was in my parents' shoes. I would like to believe I would have given a polite "no thank you" and closed the door.

Unravel

When I was a little girl, I often dreamed about being a ballerina. I'm sure a lot of girls fanaticize about the same thing. It just looked so glamorous. Not like my life at all. I wanted to be someone and somewhere else. I wanted so bad to be graceful and beautiful as I imagined ballet dancers to be. I am sure so many people reading this saw themselves up on stage being cheered on by an adoring crowd, when truthfully they were really in their bedrooms wishing they didn't have such a hard life.

What I can tell you now and in my own words is that our family often lived under difficult circumstances. Not all things were bad but life could be pretty harsh. What I do know is that when I was old enough to be conscious of the world and my surroundings, I was not happy much of the time. I just know that I longed for a closeness to my mother who I could never seem to reach. Perhaps it was my family's strict religious view of the world that kept us at arm's-length. I just know that longing has had a profound impact on me and on the way I interact with my children. That doesn't mean that my mother did not love me, but there was always a wall of separation that I did not fully understand.

At times, like all children, I was carefree but my playgroup was always small. There were three of us in the little group that I did have. There was always my sister, our friend Layla, and I. We got by with what we had and seemed to have fun. We did not have a big extended family with a lot of cousins. We always stuck to ourselves.

My sister and I grew apart around the time she entered high school. However, when we were smaller, I remember sitting up late at night and talking to her about the things that bothered us or things our parents wouldn't talk to us about. We would try to figure out the world the best we could because our mother was never going to be the type of mom that would be our friend. Because my sister Marella was older I looked up to her and asked her opinion about things.

Even as children, Marella seemed to be more religious and much less prone to go against the authority imposed by a strict interpretation of the Bible. Still to this day, she is much more guided by a religious view that some might find restrictive. That isn't to say I don't have a bit of a religious bent myself. I do view the world from the religious teachings that I was raised with. I just strayed away from them at some point but in the last year have gravitated back to the church. It has provided me with a great deal of solace.

I also remember idolizing my brother Travis, Jr. I tried to follow him around, but he would always get away from me.

I didn't think to ask why a 17-year-old would want a five-year-old hanging around in the first place. I was left feeling hurt and rejected when he tried to ditch me or made me go back home. Even so, like a little puppy, I followed him around the neighborhood anyway. I just wanted some time and attention from someone to whom I felt close.

Unfortunately, Travis, Jr. and I are still distant to this day. Part of it is our age gap. We are just different people who grew up at different times. There are other reasons, but I would be incorrect to say we don't love each other. It is just difficult to have a relationship when you feel like you don't really know a person.

Because there wasn't a large extended family there were no big holiday gatherings that I can remember. For the most part, there were only three cousins that I knew well and one aunt. I'm still close to them today.

We were and still are a church-going family. I was christened and baptized at Greater Saint Paul Missionary Baptist Church in Durham. Our family would later switch churches and attend Mount Zion Christian Church. When I was about 10-years-old, it was one of the first large nondenominational mega-churches in the area and its congregation is probably several thousand. Mt Zion is probably best known for its private school and its nationally recognized prep basketball teams, which had players who have gone on to become big NBA stars.

Beyond basketball, Mount Zion Christian Church was and is still known as a place with very strict religious teachings. The members of the congregation are known throughout the area for their strict adherence to the doctrines taught by their pastor. Mount Zion had been affiliated with the Baptist Church but the church founder felt that even the Baptist were not strict enough and broke away in 1984 to form his 43,000 square foot mega-church just up the street from NCCU and only blocks from the Forestview development where we lived for a time. The pastor and church members take the Bible literally. I was raised to believe in a strict interpretation of the Bible so it is that kind of upbringing that made me fear God.

The idea of "being in the world" or having a boyfriend, things I wanted, were things that would be considered off limits for people who were members of the church. As I grew older, I wanted to rebel against the strictness of the environment in my house and at Mount Zion. My sister bought into them wholeheartedly and embraced that kind of religion. I found it stifling and wanted to test the limits. You could make the case that even though the religious teaching didn't allow for much freedom, the teachings would have kept me from going too far off the track. Whenever I've been tempted to do certain things, the sermons of pastor would still be ringing in my ear.

Church services were the center of our family's social schedule. We didn't have game night or go to the Star-Lite drive-in like other families did. That was something that I longed for. Because we didn't have that kind of family time, with my children now I try to provide some balance and allow them to do things outside of church.

So you can see that my dream about being a ballet dancer didn't fit so nicely with the way our parents went about raising us. Whenever I said something about dance, even being a ballerina, my family thought I should consider something else.

They would tell me things like I should consider being a lawyer or something else because real people didn't make a living dancing. I am starting to think that maybe I was destined to do the kind of dancing that was distorted and led to a less than honorable lifestyle. A lifestyle filled with choices that would lead to decisions that I would later come to regret. Because being a ballerina was never a real possibility for me.

My sister had always expressed an interest in being a teacher. However, everyone in the family told her she should grow up to be a doctor. There seemed to be a level of support for what she did that was not extended to me. Marella had always appeared to be working hard and her grades never suffered. The adults around us were quick to praise everything she did. She also never seemed to do anything to make herself look bad in the eyes of the adults around us. I don't remember her getting in any of kind of trouble. Everyone, including me, thought she was very intelligent and would go far in life.

I felt I was the complete opposite of my sister. I couldn't figure out why people thought I wasn't capable of living out my dreams while they openly had so much confidence in my sister. I didn't want to believe that my parents saw me as different or were treating me unfairly. It was clear to me that when I was young, the adults around me were having a strong influence on what I would later become without knowing it. There had never been any support for any of the things I dreamed about. Even as they expressed a desire for me to be something, it was never what I envisioned myself.

A bonus for Marella was that she was driven and focused. I, on the other hand, always felt uninspired.

This causes me to think about my own children. I don't ever want them to believe they cannot do something meaningful with their lives. Even so, I don't want to decide what my children will be either. Sadly, some parents stop supporting their children when they do not live up to the parent's dreams. In turn the child gives up on his or her dream when their parents stop supporting them. That was my case. I felt that since no one seemed to care what I did, I would downgrade my expectations. There was no way I was going to be a ballerina so there was no way I was going to be anything else either. I'm not saying that was a conscious choice. Many of the decisions I would make in my life were bad ones; not just mistakes, but unconscious attempts to self-sabotage any success I might have had. My dreams of dancing on stage in a serious ballet were never going to happen if there was no one there to encourage me to reach my goals. On account of my rebellious actions, I would never put myself in a position for anything good to happen. Of course the irony is that I am known as a dancer—an exotic dancer. I have the label on me and I want to get it off. Even as I stood on stage at the Platinum Pleasures Club, I continued to imagine myself being respected for what I did long after it was clear that my life had taken a wrong turn. What I ended up doing was considered sex work, and I clearly didn't expect to be doing that kind of dancing. My plan is to never go back.

While thinking about my childhood I wonder if it is sadder to be the adult who has given up on childhood dreams or to be the parents who have given up on their children because they can only think about how disappointed they are that their offspring turned out to be something less. I have to live with both because I'm sure I have caused some embarrassment and made news for all the wrong reasons. That is surely disappointing for my parents. I don't believe they have ever given up on me.

I certainly feel regret because it seems I have been forever unable to please myself or others as I've continued to be self-destructive. I wasn't a child whose parents signed them up for everything that I really did not want to do. Things could have turned out differently for me if I could have seen the advantages that I had. I didn't have to worry about my parents putting tremendous pressure on me to perform up to a standard that I was not willing or capable of achieving. If I had been able to seize on my own initiative and think only about my own goals, I perhaps could have had a real dance career. At least I can remember what my childhood dream was.

Based on what I know about my life, I worry about other little girls growing up today.

I suspect more African American girls growing up today would desire to be a singer, model, or dancer based on the constant stream of video vixens paraded before them. There isn't much chance that you will hear expressions of a desire to be a doctor, lawyer, or ballerina in our communities. That is something I want to see changed. I have been able to see close up the results of our inability or unwillingness to encourage all of our girls to aim for higher positions in life.

I know some women out there who are living positive lives, and I do not mean to paint with a very broad brush. However, most of the women I worked with as an exotic dancer and escort had never had stability in their lives. I don't think they could even tell you what they dreamed about becoming. Even if they could, they were all adversely influenced by the images they saw. Women in the sex entertainment industry are just a shade different than the women you see in the videos. Consequently, instead of living up to an image of a successful and respected woman, everyone I encountered was in reality mimicking the most pervasive images each saw. They were living down far below what they were capable of achieving. Doing drugs, selling themselves for others' pleasure all because they envision no better life for themselves.

Still today, the emphasis on beauty and looks has too much influence. Non-average women set the standard for the vast majority of us. Women who wear sizes that we never wore and never will are the ones who control the clothes hanging on the racks. We try to squeeze into those clothes thinking we will be as beautiful as the pictures in the magazine. After all, our ticket to success is punched if we are beautiful in the eyes of the public.

When I was a little girl, I would imagine myself in the body of Janet Jackson, Paula Abdul, or Mariah Carey. I think that now young girls are hoping they can look and be like Britney Spears, Paris Hilton, or Lindsay Lohan. We all know what those three have been going through. Their struggles with their sexual image, weight, drugs and alcohol are not something we should want our daughters to suffer from, but they are the biggest stars.

It was no secret that as a young girl I struggled to fit in. It was obvious that Tyra Banks would never have picked me to be "America's Next Top Model." As a teenager and starting to develop, I came in at 5'4" and nothing like the 5'11 super model types. I was dark-skinned and didn't have the features people associated with beauty. In addition to that, I was flat-chested and had narrow hips.

Because I struggled with my self-image, I spent a lot of time by myself, often dancing alone in front of the television. When I was doing that I felt vivacious, alive and free. Dancing provided me hope and an escape. Dancing was life. It represented to me more than just movement; it was spiritual and came from deep down in my soul. It made me think about how I could rise above all of the pressures of everyday life. I could be like a caterpillar emerging from a cocoon to be a butterfly. On the other hand, I could just leap for joy whenever I felt like it. There were no restrictions.

Because my parents were never going to send me for formal dance lessons and most of the time we never could afford it, watching music videos was my teacher. I would sit for hours at a time, transfixed by the images. Day after day, watching every music video, I was studying every move as if I was in a choreography class. After my marathon television-watching sessions were over, I'd spend more hours practicing the latest moves. I worked hard at perfecting the routines until my performances were mirror images of what the music videos had portrayed. I never intended for those performances to be seen by anyone. Nevertheless, as fate would have it, those routines would later become the core of the dance routines I performed on stage at the Platinum Pleasures Club.

I believe many girls do the same thing that I did. They use the images in the music videos and pop culture as their guide. They internalize what they see and live through those images. They take the words in the songs to heart. I did the same thing. Those songs provided the rhythm and the poetry of my life. My body and mind responded to the high pitches, low beats, and the words to every song.

Dancing still is and will always be a way to release from difficult circumstances that are beyond my control. Sometimes, I felt I had entered a state of grace—a place where I was at peace.

Despite the fact that my father worked hard to make more money, we were never going to be more than a working-class family. We had grown accustomed to the short-lived but highly impressionable glamorous life that the settlement money offered. It didn't last nearly long enough. We were even going without much needed things. I know my parents were doing the absolute best they could. The times returned when my dad was hardly at home. When he was there, he retreated to the garage where he was working on cars for payment he expected the following day. A lot of people didn't pay him. There was always, "I don't have the money today. I'll get you next week when I have some money."

Then the arguments erupted between my parents. My dad would say things would be easier if my mom got a job to help out with the bills. I sympathized with my mom who had always been a housewife. I know it would have been a great relief for my father had my mother been able to contribute. He was right; we needed her to work to help the family. My mom had always taken care of us while my father worked.

She felt that was her role and that alone was enough and an occupation in its own right.

I wanted to ask them both if they ever listened to each other. Maybe the more important question was whether they understood each other. Surely, my mother saw the situation we were in. However, I was a child and knew not to stick my nose where it didn't belong. I always thought there was an answer to our problems if they would just stop making things so complicated and open up to each other.

With the bills mounting and our financial situation reverting back to where we had been when the insurance ran out, I started to feel anxious and depressed. I wanted to talk to my mother, but I didn't think she had a clue about how I felt or what I was going through internally. My body was starting to change in addition to everything else, and I wanted to know what was going on but my mother and father never thought it was important to talk about those kinds of things with the children.

The few times I did ask questions about my body, my mother would say, "You have plenty of time for that, just concentrate on your school work." That was the end of the discussion with her, but that didn't dampen my curiosity.

I thought about the moms I saw on television and it always seemed they were doing makeup with their daughters, talking about important issues, and discussing their femininity. Nevertheless, I knew that wasn't going to happen at my house and with my mother, so I turned to my dad.

"Daddy," I asked, "why is mom so different?"

My father explained that there had been some things that had happened in her life that made her feel uncomfortable talking about the very things I wanted to know. It made my mother worry more than she should have, and she believed she was protecting me from the world. I did not understand what my dad was trying to tell me at the time, and I was left feeling more confused and alienated from my mother then ever.

My father reminded me of an incident that happened with my mother that had shaken all of us. On a warm sunny Saturday afternoon, my sister and I were lying on the living room in front of the big floor model television watching cartoons. Dad was in the garage working on cars. Our brother was around the corner playing basketball with some of the neighborhood boys. My sister and I were startled by a blood-curdling cry coming from the kitchen.

We jumped up to see what was going on. Mother was standing in the center of the kitchen screaming and crying until her voice started to fade because she was growing hoarse. We stood in shocked silence as our father followed her as she paced back and forth with a cigarette clinched tightly in her fisted hand. I glanced down and notice a pile of ashes on the floor. An ashtray was shattered into a hundred pieces on the kitchen floor.

With concern written on his face, my father reached for my mother to embrace and comfort her. Every time, she would pull away. The scene both saddened and frightened me. I was so overwhelmed I began to cry. During this episode my mother began to shout, "Help! Help me Lord! I need help!" But this wasn't like anything she had ever done in church or around the house. She shook uncontrollably and screamed even louder.

I wanted to rush over and embrace my mother just as my father was trying to do. I wanted to help her, and I wanted this to stop. I was small, powerless, and afraid. I cried out, "Daddy, help Mommy!"

The sound of my voice caught my father off guard. During all of the commotion he did not realize that my sister and I had been standing there watching. Stunned and speechless, he took us to our room without offering any comments and he returned to the kitchen to comfort our mother.

After things calmed down, my sister and I found ourselves in the emergency room with our aunt. She watched us while my dad accompanied my mother to see the psychiatrist. We bombarded our aunt with questions. "What's wrong with Mommy? Is she okay? Why is she acting like that?"

I did not think she knew what to say. The only thing people ever say at a time like this is, "Your mother will be fine," and she said that. But she went on to add, "Don't be afraid if you don't see your mother for some time. She might have to stay so that they can help her recover, but she will be okay."

Much to everyone's surprise, they let us back to visit with my mother before we left the hospital. We all crowded anxiously together into a small, secured room somewhere in the hospital. We all stood there not sure what to say. I decided to be bold and break the silence. "Mom, are you better now?"

My mother reached towards me but did not say anything. She made a gesture as if she was holding her breath. The smell in the room was that peculiar hospital smell, only stronger. She leaned back.

"It's okay, Mom. You will be fine because God knows we need you." I knew my mother had faith, and I wanted to offer her comfort in a way I thought she could understand. Seeing her in that condition made me appreciate her more. Despite the fact she wasn't like the television moms, she was my mother. There was a reason why she was the way she had been. Perhaps her stay in the hospital could fix things. From that moment, I cherished every opportunity to be with my mother no matter the circumstance, because the alternative was for her not to be here at all and I didn't ever want that to happen.

Being a child, the thought of my mother being away, even if she needed help, was not a comfort. We were already struggling and now our mother was going to be gone for who knows how long. Not only would our father have to find a way for us to survive financially, he would have to take care of everything else as well.

That day at the hospital with my mother became imprinted in my memory. It is hard seeing your parents not able to take care of themselves, because that means they cannot take care of you either. I was not yet 10, but I was already familiar with how vulnerable and frail humans can be. My father suffered physically and my mother mentally. Years later my vulnerabilities and frailties would also be revealed. However mine would be shared with the entire nation and under circumstances that no person would ever wish on their worst enemy.

In spite of my naiveté, I knew something had caused my mother's irrational behavior. She wasn't crazy. She was being tormented. There had been years of abuse and neglect building up that led to her breakdown. To this day she is suffering and there still isn't anything I can do about it.

I later learned about her past. As a little girl, she was forced to sit on her daddy's knee, but she was there for his pleasure. She would weep because she didn't want to be there and she would retreat to the back steps of the house to find a refuge away from her painful secret. Then as a teenager her father's fondling lead to other abuses, but she was too afraid to tell her mother. If only we could have talked about her past openly, I believe I would have made better choices in my life.

Rebellion

The financial troubles that my parents faced were hard on all of us. I'm sure it had an effect on my brother and sister, but we reacted in different ways. I know that for me it made me love them all the more and not want to see them hurt. As I got older, I thought about how much they had sacrificed and tried to do for me, even if I did not repay them with the love and respect they deserved.

The times following my father's accident and my mother's breakdown were tough. My body was still changing, and I was starting to grow apart from my sister. I had always felt that Marella received better treatment than I did. I thought it was on account of her lighter skin and more manageable hair. Things my family said and the way they acted justified my belief, and I had begun to feel inferior. I found it hard to live in the home, and it forced me to make another very regrettable decision. I decided I needed to leave home and be somewhere else. I thought, perhaps, it would be better if I was on my own, but I didn't know how I could do it. I just started retreating from the family as much as I could.

Little did I know that the slights I received there would be nothing in comparison to what I would face trying to make relationships with people who truly do not care about me.

I know now that I had no business demanding so much attention. I certainly can see that my emotions were out of control, and negatively influenced every action and decision. Even though some in my family and society believed that lighter meant better I should have realized that they could not determine my worth. It is a hard task for a teenage girl to figure out that her worth is inside and not out. It was next to impossible to feel the love expressed by my parents and to recognize that their love should have been enough to overcome my feelings of inadequacy.

My rage against all of the slights from my sister would finally come to a head. I had to lash out in some way to relieve the tension that had been building up for so long.

One morning the alarm clock rang. It was my sister's alarm clock; I did not have one of my own. I decided to get up before my sister and avoid her. I grabbed a T-shirt and a pair of jean shorts from my dresser as quietly as I could. As I made my way to the bathroom, I suddenly realized I had left my towel and underwear in the bedroom. I would have to go back and open my squeaky dresser drawer to get my things. That would surely wake my sister, but I didn't have a choice. As I tried to gingerly pull the drawer out, my sister woke and sprang up from the bed. "No, I'm first!" she shouted. "Now wait for your turn."

I was incensed. "My things are already in the bathroom! I was up before you!"

My sister completely ignored me, stormed out of the room, and headed straight for my dad's room. He was fast asleep but she woke him anyway. Neither to my surprise nor liking, my father took her side, and I was relegated to waiting for her to go in first and finish at her own leisure.

I found myself waiting quietly on the edge of my bed. As each moment passed, it grew harder to suppress the hurt and anger. The tears built up slowly but ran in streams down my cheeks.

"I hate her," is all I could think. I fought the urge to think more about hating my sister. I wanted to love her. I did love her. The problem was the hurt of constantly being disrespected was just too much for me to take. I honestly tried to hide and suppress the feelings I had towards my sister but this was too much. Such a petty thing like who took a shower first was foul play and needed a response. To involve our father and for him to take her side was worse than just being unfair.

So I sat there listening to the water run. I could hear the stream cascading against the shower walls. Each drop of water made my blood boil. The sound was too much. It seemed so loud it was almost hurting my ears. All in a flash my anger hit its climax. I jumped to my feet in a sudden fit of rage and vengeance. "I'll fix her," I thought. I violently ripped the sheets on her freshly made bed, stripping it bare. I whirled around and in a flash swept my sister's belongings from her dresser and onto the floor. There was shampoo splashed everywhere as a nearly full bottle crashed to the floor, splattering its contents. I surveyed the mess and felt satisfied that her ruined possessions looked as bad as I felt. I had gotten some revenge.

The feeling of satisfaction quickly went away as I heard my mother making her way down the hall. She frantically called to my father, "What was that noise?" It was going to be just a matter of minutes before they would see what I had done. I wouldn't have time to pick things up, and I would not be able to make any excuses for what I had done. All the feeling of anger washed away as I tried to figure out what to do next.

My only option would be to hide. My dad's footsteps sound as if he was running. I could tell he was angry just hearing him rush towards the room. I slipped quickly into the closet. It was the only place I could go to provide a temporary haven from my father.

My father burst through the door just as I managed to hide beneath a pile of clothes. "What in the world? Who did this?"

Just then my sister entered to room. "What, Daddy? What happened?" There was no question that I been the one who turned the room upside down and caused so much chaos. "Spank her daddy for ruining my things," she cried.

Amid all of the commotion I surveyed the scene from my hiding place beneath the pile of clothes. I watched silently in the hopes of not being found but that was unlikely. There were only a few places I could have been, but I hoped anyway. My father looked in the first place anyone would be in these circumstances—underneath the bed. He poked his head underneath cautiously as if he had expected to be attacked by a wild animal. There was nothing. He turned and looked behind the partially closed bedroom door. He peeked slowly and moved cautiously as if he was expecting a surprise or shock. My heart started to race as he came to the only other place I could be hiding. I had been careless and forgot to fully close the door and cover my feet. He spotted me right away. He quickly snatched me from the pile of clothes by my feet.

I screamed uncontrollably as a belt swung towards me. I tried to brace myself for the first lash and grabbed at the weapon at the same time. My father gripped the strap tightly and swung with tremendous force. There was no way I was going to stop this beating. I could feel the whelps springing up all over my body with each blow.

"It wasn't my fault," I protested. "Daddy, please! Daddy, please don't. I'm sorry. I won't do it again!" My cries for mercy would be of no use. I suspect he did not hear anything I was saying. He continued to beat me along my back and my legs. The sting was unbearable and I couldn't escape.

When the beating stopped, my father turned and left the room without a word. I could only kneel right where I was and continue to cry. Instead of the anger and vindication that I felt only moments ago, I was now feeling lonely and misunderstood. "Why is everyone always so angry at me and what did I do to deserve this?"

The thoughts of the beating I had just suffered lingered. The pain from the leather strap throbbed and reminded me why I had wanted to destroy my sister's things in the first place. I thought about all the other slights I had to suffer at her hands. I tried to think about dancing. I heard music playing in my head and tried to concentrate on how that made me feel. I needed to be free from this.

But my sister could not leave well enough alone. She mumbled under her breath, "That's what you get. That's why everyone is always taking my side. You are a nobody." She rubbed more salt into my wounds.

Her insults took over my mind. I didn't hear music any more. I wasn't dancing. I visualized my father swinging the leather belt at me. Destroying my sister's things was not going to be enough, I thought. I had to strike back at her and make her hurt physically like I had been hurt. With her back turned, I rushed her and grabbed the back of her head. She was able to grab me, but I struggled and was able to pull away. We were separated but now my sister had an opportunity to attack.

All of a sudden, she was charging at me and yelling, "I hate you! I'm going to kill you." Hearing those words, I felt my sister's fingernails dig into the skin on my face. I could feel the blood running down my cheek in streams. Immediately, I recognized that my face would be scared and so this fight was far from over. It could not end with her getting the best of me.

As I regained my composure and tried to launch a counter attack, my father reentered the room. I was outnumbered and sent reeling again. I saw that my father came swinging the same leather belt that he had just used to subdue me. My first instinct was to grab at it and to prevent him from beating me again. To my amazement I was able to get my father off balance and push him to the floor. My victory didn't last long as my brother made his first appearance. He joined the fray and took the side of my father and sister. Before I could react, my brother had me firmly in a choke hold. I struggled against him but I couldn't resist any longer. My sister and father would easily be able to take me down, even if I was able to break away from my brother's grasp. It was no use to keep fighting. I was defeated and in a total in a state of exhaustion. I surrendered.

The fight with my sister was a defining moment for me. It put me on a path of pursuing happiness and love in all the wrong places. I was convinced that my family did not love me. They were against me, and they would not and could not treat me as equal to my sister.

Strangely, I felt stronger after the incident. I had fought back. Even though I had not won, I thought it was a sign that I was more mature for not letting them get away with hurting me without saying anything. Of course it was wrongheaded, but I was only 14. I believed I was old enough to know how to deal with the feelings I was having. There was an easier answer to my problems than trying to fight with them. I could just pick up and go away. Leaving my family would be easy because I didn't need them for anything. I decided that running away from home would be the best course of action. I didn't do it that day but the wheels were set in motion. I would endure some other problems at home and school and lose my best friend before I acted out, but in my mind the day of the fight was my last day as part of my family.

It is really scary for me knowing that I have to raise two daughters in a world where kids beat each other up on YouTube and genuinely think nothing of it. Imagine the kind of trouble a girl can get into when she doesn't believe there is anyone at home to love and care for her.

Since that incident and around the time I started high school, I felt mad all the time. I have largely put out of my mind elementary and middle school because I can only remember how cruel kids were to the ones like me who did not fit in.

"I wish I was beautiful," I would say to myself. At age 14 I felt like a little girl among grownup women. I did not look much different from when I was 10-years-old, even though I felt changes within. Hillside High School was not an easy place if you weren't a part of one of the cliques or a cool person or an attractive girl. I felt like I was none of those things.

Hillside High, one of the largest schools in North Carolina, is almost 100 percent black. I felt lost there when I listened in on girls' conversations. I didn't know about boys and the other things they talked about. I still had never been able to talk to my mother. My father was now off limits after the fight with my sister.

For me it was impossible to even think about trying to keep up in fashion or appearances. With no money to buy the latest clothes, I had no sense of what was cool or hip. My confidence had been completely shattered.

As a result, I would sit back and watch. "I wish I was beautiful," I told myself because I couldn't see how anyone could think that about me. Every time I looked in the mirror, I saw the same boyish figure. I wore the same cheap clothes that my parents picked out for me that would not flatter me.

The one thing I continued to do was retreat to my room with the radio or music videos and dance. Only then did it not matter if I was popular or pretty. But the private dancing only offered temporary relief.

I needed to find another way to express myself. I turned to my schoolwork, and poured my energy into my books. I could be smart if I wasn't going to be beautiful. Shortly, I was making the best grades I had ever made. My parents complemented me on the change and expressed their surprise at how well I was doing.

Soon I was on the "A" honor roll and getting attention for my accomplishments. I remember vividly the awards ceremony in front of the school where I was recognized along with some others for making significant progress during the semester, and led the procession into the assembly. I was the student who had made the most progress overall. I was so happy; I was finally first at something.

Being one of the "smart kids" gave me entry into a whole new social set—the nerds. The feeling of belonging was very different. I was at ease for a change and thought that maybe I had turned a corner.

I turned my focus completely to getting good grades and dancing. Nothing else was going to matter as long as I had the incentive to make good grades. As long as I could not be compared negatively to my sister, I could be on a level playing field. This gave me a measure of control over my life and each reporting period made things seem that much better.

I was still consumed by wanting to look better. I would stare into the mirror, wishing my body would somehow morph right in front of me if I looked long and hard enough.

Right when things were going better for me, I was dealt a serious blow. Nothing like my dad's accident or my mom's breakdown but something that would hurt me and have a lasting impact on how I viewed friendship.

One very hot morning before school, I awoke to my father holding an ice-cold washcloth to my face. The alarm clock buzzed in the background. "You're late," my father said.

My mother was asleep as usual and my sister sat nearby already dressed and prepared to go to school.

"I don't feel good, Daddy," I said, pleading my case.

"If you don't go to school, you can't go anywhere else today or the rest of this week," he said firmly.

I knew my father meant what he said. I struggled out of bed and to my feet. I had to find something to wear in a hurry but my clothes were strewn all over the room. I could not tell what was clean or dirty.

I got there just in time for first period. As I was rushing, I caught a glimpse of one of the few friends I did have at school. She was the only person I felt like I could talk to and by far the best friend I had ever had. Her name was Nikita. She rushed past me as if I was not even there. "Hi Nikita! Come here," I yelled.

"I'm late," Nikita shot back. "I'll see you later."

Nikita always found time to talk to me whether we were running late for class or not. This was strange behavior on her part. It made me wonder if she was having trouble at home. Frequently when her mother was dating a new man, Nikita would not be her usual self. During those times when she was angry with her mother, she would still talk to me. I was an outlet for her just as she had been one for me. We understood each other and there was no holding back our feelings and there were no fears when we talked.

The encounter with Nikita left me shaken. Had I done something to hurt her feelings? There was too much at stake to let it slide by so easily. It was only nine in the morning and there wouldn't be another chance to see her for some time. I was going to have to wait three hours before I would see my friend, and it felt like a lifetime.

As the bell rang for lunch, I quickly retrieved my book bag and waited for the teacher to give the signal that we could leave the room. I needed to get to the library. Nikita and I always met in the library and avoided the cafeteria like the plague. There was no point in us going to the cafeteria anyway because we were misfits and were looked upon with scorn when we did go. The library was a safe haven for us.

I felt a sense of sadness because she wasn't there at our favorite table. There was only one other place she could be. We sometimes retreated to our quiet spot behind the school where no one else would go. I sprinted to our spot, but she wasn't there either. Now, I was really starting to worry that something was seriously wrong. I decided to go back to the library one last time to check.

I straightened my back and concentrated on not showing any outward signs of emotion.

At first I did not notice my sister and a couple of her friends sitting at a table. It was taking all of my energy to avoid looking like I was upset. Marella knew that Nikita was my only true friend and if I was having lunch without her, I was definitely a loser. It would be far too embarrassing to be seen without my friend. My sister would have a field day teasing me about being alone.

I found a spot by the magazine rack, made a selection and sat down. Out of the corner of my eye, I could see a small figure approaching. It was Michelle and she was making a beeline for my table. I knew her because we had a few classes together.

Michelle sat down at the table uninvited, and I didn't say anything. I just looked in my magazine as if I did not see her. What could she possibly want? She did not look at me, keeping her head down. What could she possibly want with me?

We sat there awkwardly for some time. When it appeared she was not going to be the one to break the silence, I leaned over to whisper, "Hi Michelle, have you seen Nikita?"

Michelle turned away from staring at my magazine and looked at nothing in particular. She did so as if to purposely not look into my eyes when she responded nonchalantly to me, "Yeah, she's coming."

We sat there uncomfortably as the time ticked by. It was almost time for the next class bell. It was weird sitting there with Michelle and not saying anything.

I had given up all hope when I looked up and there was Nikita standing outside of the window of the library. I hurriedly got my things together and rushed to meet her. Michelle got up at the same time and walked with me to the door. I was so happy to see my friend that I could feel the smile on my face. When I got outside the door, I spoke and my friend acted as though she did not hear or see me.

There were other kids in the hall, but I did not hear a single sound. I was fixated on Nikita and waiting for her to respond to my greeting. There was no response. My best friend turned to Michelle and greeted her warmly like I expected her to do to me. They launched into a conversation as if they were the best of friends and I wasn't even there.

I couldn't believe this was happening. Should I risk making a bigger fool of myself by trying to talk to Nikita? "Were you in the lunch room? Did you go outside?" I asked excitedly.

The two girls looked at each other and smiled, as if they were party to some inside joke. I could never imagine that Nikita, of all people, would turn her back on me. I stood there with my heart beneath my feet as they walked away without saying another word. Just like that, Michelle managed to take away one of the sure things I had. Now I had another reason not to trust anyone.

Over the next few days, I watched Nikita closely. I wanted to see just what happened to make her change so drastically. She didn't resemble the person I had come to know and love at all. I was so angry and wanted to lash out at her. I thought about all the ugly names I could call her, but I knew that wouldn't do any good. What I really wanted to do was to tell her how much I missed her and wanted to do anything to get back into her good graces. Nikita was now hanging out with the very girls that ridiculed me.

I can truly say my friendship with Nikita was the most important relationship I had from middle school to the early part of high school. We had sleepovers and birthday parties at each other's house. Our moms took turns looking after the both of us. How could she forget such special moments like the ones we had shared? Confused and feeling alone again, I sank back into a depression.

My relationship with Nikita had been a buffer that allowed me to keep some distance away from my problems at home. I was still at odds with my family. Getting good grades wasn't going to be enough to help me deal with the loss of my best friend and the hornets' nest at home. I was going to have to find another outlet and look for something else to cover up my pain.

Somehow I made it through the rest of that terrible school day, but I let all of the sadness come spilling out at home. I sat in my room crying into my pillow, unaware of time. My eyes were puffy, my nose ran freely, and there were tears still flowing down my face as I arrived at the dinner table.

Sadly, not one word was directed to me about why I looked so distressed. Could it really be that not a single soul in my family cared anything at all about me and would not try to console me in the least?

My sister took command of the dinner table as she did every night, torturing us with stories about how great she was at school that day. She would not stop talking so I made her disappear in my mind. I stared off into space.

I started thinking about *why* my parents loved each one of us. They loved my sister because she was smart, good-looking, and was going to do things with her life. They loved my brother because he was dedicated and hardworking like my dad. Me on the other hand—I was nothing but trouble. I was sullen, resentful, and fought back. I had a chip on my shoulder that had so many causes. Chief among them was the hurt I felt because people found me unattractive. The conclusion I reached was that my parents reluctantly loved me. It was by default: I was their child and they had no choice but to love me.

Back in my room, I thought that home was no better for me than school. The only thing I could do was pray for better circumstances, though this had not worked for me in the past.

"Oh God, please send me a special friend who won't leave me in order to become popular. Send me a new mother who will understand me. Give me a father who will not always be away from home. I wish for a new sister and brother who would at least act like they wanted me around," I prayed in earnest.

With that prayer, I wiped my tears and prepared for bed. I believed in God but He was not looking so good in my eyes right now. The thought of doubting God made me cry again. This day had been too much, and I cried myself asleep.

Meeting the Devil

My freshman year was not turning out to be anything like I had hoped. I never dreamed that things could actually get worse, but they would. A chance encounter while leaving school one day set me back even further than where I was.

Because my father had once again failed to pick up my sister and me from school, we were forced to walk home. I stopped at the edge of the schoolyard and let her walk ahead of me and fade into the distance. I walked slowly because I felt tired plus I saw no need to rush to get home.

I stepped into the intersection in front of the school to cross the street. A truck slowly approached. I wasn't sure the driver was going to stop so I froze in my tracks. I looked around to figure out how much time I would have to cross and, to my surprise, Nikita was standing beside me.

The sight of Nikita caught me off guard for a moment. I was just so happy to see Nikita. My first thought was that maybe she wanted to make up. Maybe she just didn't know what to say.

As the truck pulled along beside us, I noticed immediately that there were four guys in the truck. They were whistling and making catcalls, and I assumed they were looking at Nikita. I assumed she was the center of the attention but to my surprise one of the men leaned out of the truck and directed his attention towards me. I made one of the biggest mistakes of my life when I didn't walk away. That afternoon, I met Frederick Thomas.

"Hey, what's up, girl? Where are you going?" Frederick asked.

I stood there transfixed. I felt a grin come over my face.

This boy was talking directly to me and not Nikita. "Do you need a ride, somewhere?"

I was tempted, but I knew better. If my mother and father found out I was riding with a group of strange men, I would be in a world of trouble. "That's okay," I replied.

Frederick looked at me from head-to-toe. "Come closer and let me talk to you girl." His funny accent indicated he was not from around here. I learned later he was from the Caribbean.

Something about him was seductive, and I moved closer to the truck. All my inhibitions went away as the sensation of being noticed made me feel warm all over. I was completely trusting as I gave no thought that he or the other men might have meant me harm. I was overwhelmed because no boy and certainly no man had ever looked so intensely at my body and into my eyes. Frederick spoke to me. "Do you have a phone and can I call you?"

Without hesitation I gave Frederick my phone number. I was floating on a cloud as the truck disappeared.

Nikita had been standing on the other side of the street and watched my encounter with Frederick. I rushed across the street to tell her about what happened because it seemed as though she had been waiting for me.

"Hi." It was the first time we had spoken in months. I was out of breath with excitement. "How are you?"

"I'm okay," Nikita replied back. It was as if we had never stopped talking to each other. Nikita never said one word about the incident in the library or gave an explanation about her behavior. I didn't want to bring it up because I was afraid that I would hear something I didn't want to hear. Nikita was back in my life and a boy actually asked for my phone number. We continued to walk home together and were so caught up in our conversation that we didn't realize we were approaching Nikita's street. She took a left and I continued on to my uncle's house. My sister and I usually went there when our father forgot to pick us up.

All of a sudden, I was overcome with a feeling of dread. I had just given a stranger my phone number and let Nikita back into my life without challenging her for hurting me. Could the guys in the truck be following me? Did Nikita talk to me just to get into my business and use what she saw against me? Now I was concerned.

When I got inside my uncle's house, I saw that my sister was indeed already there. I felt even more relieved that she had not gone home without me, where she would have made a big deal about my not being with her. Of course she had already called ahead and made up a story that I was being held in detention. Consequently, it was a surprise for my father when he arrived a few minutes later to see me sitting waiting for him.

Under normal circumstances, I would have been angry with my sister for lying about my whereabouts. It didn't matter this time because I could reflect back on something positive. I had met a boy, he paid attention to me, and he even asked for my number. I felt like I did when I was dancing. Not knowing any better I immediately connected the feelings I was having with love. I was feeling that now for the first time. I just might be in love with Frederick. It didn't matter that I didn't know the first thing about him. I had no concept of dating and relationships. This was as close to being with a boy as I had ever been.

Marella and I climbed into our station wagon. My sister sat in the front as she always did. I did not feel the least bit resentful this time. That meant I would be in the back and could concentrate on replaying my meeting Frederick repeatedly, without interruption. I smiled uncontrollably at my good fortune. Wow, someone noticed me.

When we arrived at home, it was already time for dinner. We were running late and my mother was not happy at all. We were told to wash up and sit at the table. The meal seemed to go at a faster pace than normal. My sister still talked about how great she had done at school that day, my brother talked about his job, and I said nothing. After dinner they disappeared into their separate directions. It was just like every other dinner we had.

Shortly after we ate, my sister began to watch television. I'm pretty sure my brother went off to play basketball. I had stuff to do for school, so I went to do my homework. I completed my homework and got ready for bed. Then it hit me that I had given Frederick my number. I thought, "Would he really call me? What could he possibly have to say to me?" I figured it was all just a joke, and perhaps they were getting their kicks out of making me think that anyone would want to talk to me.

I had been in bed for some time when the phone rang. Something told me that it was Frederick. I was going to be in big trouble if it was because it was 10 p.m. The phone was not supposed to ring after 8:00 pm for any of the children. My mother answered the phone.

"Excuse me," my mother said. "Just who are you and how do you know Crystal?"

Apparently there was an answer on the other end. Frederick was going along with my mother's line of questions.

"From school," she shot back sarcastically. "And just how long have you known her? Where do you live? Did she tell you never to call after eight? What time do you go to bed?"

The questions came in rapid succession. Apparently he was answering to my mother's satisfaction. I heard her ask one last couple of questions about why he lived so far away and still attended the same school. I was shocked when she handed the phone over to me without asking me a single question.

It was Frederick on the other end. I didn't know what to say. I had never had a conversation with a boy like this. Frederick knew exactly what he wanted to talk about. In the almost two hours we talked, his conversation was focused—sex.

Almost immediately Frederick told me how much he wanted to lick me down there. He wanted to taste me and show how good he could make me feel. I had no clue about oral sex, but he told me not to worry he was an expert. He made every woman he was with feel good. He could do it for 24 hours straight and make me feel like a woman. He would teach me how to accept the pleasure of his tongue. There was no way to even imagine how it would feel to be with a man. I was a virgin and I tried to make my body feel the sensation he was talking about, but it didn't seem to make any sense. Why would he want to lick my private parts, and he had just met me? I wasn't completely naive and had heard people talking about sex but this was so hard to understand. I also knew that I had felt sensations in my own body. Perhaps if I let him rub his tongue against my vagina it would feel good.

Unexpectedly I heard a female voice giggling on the other end of the line. It was my sister who had been listening to the entire conversation.

Shocked and embarrassed, I wanted the conversation to end. Because my sister was giggling, I knew there must have been something wrong with the way Frederick was talking to me. I didn't like the new feeling I was starting to have—shame. Nevertheless, he liked me, and I had to like him back. That's how grown-ups love each other, but I couldn't process it all. "Why won't he just hang up the phone?"

"Would you like to come to my house and see my purple light?" Frederick asked.

My sister burst into laughter. She couldn't take it anymore. I couldn't believe she was still on the phone listening. She was humiliating me again. Would Frederick think I was laughing? He must have thought it was me because he kept pressing ahead, and I wasn't saying anything back. So, I decided not to reveal that my sister was the culprit. If I did, he would have been angry and maybe not called me back ever again. Nervously I told him to end the conversation. I thought my disinterest in talking about sex would keep him from bringing it up again. He asked one more time, and I again told him I was not going to come to his house. He offered an alternative instead; he would come to see me after school the next day. I supposed that was a reasonable compromise. It would allow me to get to know him, and I wouldn't have to have to talk about sex until I was ready to discuss it further. I mistakenly thought I could be in control of the situation.

I let Frederick know that he could call me anytime, but he had to be mindful of the rules about calling so late. I also told him that it would be a good idea to meet me after school. The prospects of seeing him again were so exciting that I totally forgot my sister was still listening on the other end.

The next day after school, Frederick was waiting for me beside a purple Nissan. He was taller and huskier than I imagined. I had only seen him sitting in the truck. He also looked much older. He hugged me easily as if we had done this before. My heart pounded uncontrollably as I was both nervous and excited. Almost immediately he brought up his desire to perform oral sex on me. I stood there in silence and tried to let it pass without responding. Instead he decided to ask me another question, "Would you like to go for a ride with me?"

I did not answer that question, but I knew what I wanted to do.

I had already made up my mind and I could already picture myself riding with him, but I knew it was wrong.

"What's wrong?" His questioning was not forceful. "What's your reason for not wanting to ride with me?"

"My mother would be worried," I answered. I knew she was already concerned. She wanted to know how old he was. I wanted to know the same thing. I could hear my mother's voice in my head, "You sound much older than Crystal."

I tried to ask in a way that wouldn't threaten our new relationship, "How old are you?" I was already conscious of his posture. He carried himself in a way the let me know he was authoritative and much more like a man than the boys I saw around school and my neighborhood. I had the feeling I shouldn't question him because I was taught to respect adults, but I needed to know this one thing. Something told me the age gap was much more than my parents would ever approve.

"I just turned 19," Frederick said.

It couldn't be because he definitely looked and seemed so much older. I wanted his attention so badly that I had to believe him. He was so attractive and I had already fallen for him. I pressed him again and asked straight out if he was telling me the truth because I had to know if anyone asked me.

Frederick assured me again that he was only 19. His voice was sincere and soothing. He assured me that he could not and would not do anything to hurt me. The prospect of my moving forward in this relationship was dependent on my doing something positive. If I would not let him perform oral sex on me, I would at least have to take a ride with him.

I suspended all of my concerns and got into the car with Frederick. Thinking back now, it was a completely crazy thing to do. Frederick could have easily overpowered me and done anything he wanted to me without me being able to fight back. On top of that, nobody would have the slightest clue as to where I was. My sister heard the conversation over the phone the night before. Nikita saw me talking to this man but no one knew anymore about him than I did.

As we rode, I was on top of the world. Finally, this was my chance to have someone who adored me and saw me as beautiful. He cared about me and I could adore him back as long as he treated me like the most important person on the face of the earth. He even told me he loved me right then and there and he would treat me like a queen! I had nothing to worry about.

When the car stopped in front of a house, Frederick told me his friend Marquis was there and wanted me to meet him. I sat beside Frederick on a couch. I noticed the room was filled with men who looked much older like Frederick. A heavy cloud of smoke hung over the room and the scent of reefer smoking was strong.

It was apparent that I was drawing a great deal of attention as the only girl present. It made me feel uncomfortable to see men staring at me.

I sensed that Frederick felt the same way I did concerning the looks from the other men in the room. His attitude seemed to turn defensive and angry. He let it be known to the other men in the room that I was his girlfriend. I was so taken by the jealousy he was expressing that I failed to realize that being his girlfriend would be a terrible mistake. I felt special right at the time I should have been on guard.

Frederick hung very closely to me, complementing everything about me. He told me that he loved me more than

I could ever imagine. He even offered me a token to show how much he cared; he gave me his brand new hat and a gold chain. As we were leaving his friends' house, he hugged me again, and kissed me gently on the cheek. He didn't bring up sex at this moment. Instead he told me he wanted to take things slow and get to know me better.

Leaving that house I was on cloud nine. Things were just getting better and better. I was so giddy and caught up in conversation that I didn't realize that the car had stopped. When I did finally notice we were not near my house but several blocks away. I was thinking, "Why doesn't he take me to my house?"

Without my saying a word, he offered, "I know you are wondering why I can't drop you off at your house." He didn't give me time to respond. "I know you said your mother would be worried if she knew you were with me, so it's a good idea to let you off here."

I couldn't let anyone in my family know I had been riding around with him. He told me to think up a reason why I was so late getting home. It could be because I took the city bus home and the route was much longer. I trusted that he was telling me to do the right thing because he was trying to make sure that he could love me without interference from my parents. I remained silent and reluctantly got out of the car, dreading going home. Here in Frederick's purple Nissan I was somebody special. I walked slowly away with my head down and glanced back. Frederick motioned for me to come around to his window. He held on to my hand and gazed into my eyes, "I'm glad I met you, he said." I just smiled.

Lord knows I was so young and naive. I also know that there are girls having the very same encounter everyday. Before I knew it, I was in far too deep to get out. There are many days when I wish I had listened to my mother's advice, but I thought she was trying to keep me away from something I needed. My father knew there was only a limited chance to find something good in a relationship. Neither of my parents knew how to convey the reality of love. Perhaps if there had been one caring conversation to warn me. I felt so unloved at home by my parents and siblings that I could have never made good decisions on my own.

Frederick knew from the time he saw me that I was lonely and confused. He took advantage of my lack of experience. I did not realize what true love was about and neither did he. I would have to go through a living hell with Frederick to see that even though my parents made serious mistakes raising me, they did not take me through the levels of abuse that this man would. My emotions and sensitivity had not allowed me to appreciate the things that I already had—a haven at home safe from a world filled with cruel people like Frederick.

It would not be long before my new boyfriend would show his true colors. The relationship between Fredrick and I blossomed. As we grew closer, I let down my guard and he became just Fred. We spent hour after hour on the phone, mostly talking about nothing. It didn't matter what we were saying. I finally had someone of my own. Our relationship helped me rekindle my friendship with Nikita. Fred acted as a go between and helped us work out our differences. I was willing to let things go because I had someone to occupy my time. It helped that Nikita now had a boyfriend of her own; his name was Darvis. Our relationships gave us something in common. She could talk about how things were going with Darvis and I with Fred.

Soon kids at school noticed I was in a relationship, but it was positive. However, they could tell that Fred was far too old for me. I got weird looks whenever he showed up to the school to pick me up. Nikita on the other hand never seemed to worry about the age difference. Besides, I felt comfortable with Fred and that's all that mattered to me. I had never had anyone to pay that much attention to me like this and there was no way I was going to give him up over the age difference.

I became more eager to open up to Fred, and he seemed more willing to listen. He stopped the constant sex talk for the moment, and would hear me out whenever I wanted to say something. I talked with him a lot about why I hated being at home. I told him I felt that I was either being totally ignored or always felt picked on, or that I was being fussed at for things I did not do.

Fred was always there with soothing words, "You don't need them to make you feel special. If they don't love you for who you are, then forget them."

That was incredible. Fred always managed to say exactly what I was longing to hear. How did Fred know just what to say? The more we talked, the more I wanted to be away from my family and just have Fred in my life."

Fred had taken complete control of my life in no time. He wanted me to drop everyone and everything unless he approved. That meant that sometimes I could be around Nikita but that was all. I didn't even think about dancing. It seemed childish and silly. I was to be solely around him and totally dependent. He was to be the only one I could show any affection towards or give any attention to. I was at the happiest point in my life and God had come through after all.

Despite that all seemed to be going right, the relationship was mostly about me. I wanted to know something about Fred. He said he was living with his mom that seemed reasonable if he was as young as he said he was. He also told me that he had been married with his own place, but he was divorced and the wife took their son and the house. He had gotten his ex-wife pregnant at age 17, and he did the right thing and got married to support her and the child. The only thing I could think was that he was very sweet and thoughtful, and she must have been a terrible bitch for not seeing how great a man Fred was. Fred knew how to make me feel sorry for him. I wanted to know where his family lived, I asked, "Where is you son now?"

Fred said he couldn't talk about it. The whole saga made him too emotional. It was best that we didn't discuss that any more. I bought the story, hook, line, and sinker, believing that he had gone through all he had told me. He stuck to that story about his age—19—and what his life had been like, and I had no way to prove otherwise. I could have checked his driver's license but he was so good for me, why doubt what God had provided for me.

Fred came to pick up at school more and more. I relished these moments because it gave me the opportunity to flaunt my boyfriend in front of the people who still thought I was ugly. One day when Fred came to pick me up, I remember taking my time to walk slowly to the car. I wanted to make sure I got the maximum exposure possible. I fumbled with my purse pretending I was looking for something to drag the time out even more.

Fred had gotten out to open the door for me like a gentlemen. He let me take as long as I wanted to get in the car. He was happy to make the girls feel a little envious of my man and me. He played along with me, "What did you forget?"

Everyone seemed to stand still and wait for me to answer Fred, but I said nothing and got in the car.

When I got in the car we had a good laugh and talked about how our day had been. Nothing had happened; it is what we always talked about. Of course we said how much we missed each other. Sometime during Fred's end of the conversation, I drifted off and stared out of the window. Fred continued to talk; I had completely spaced out but wasn't concentrating on anything in particular.

At the moment I realized I wasn't listening to him a young man happened to walk up along the side of the car. I paid little attention to pedestrians walking next to the car but Fred thought differently. I tried to apologize for drifting off. "I'm sorry," I said, "I think I was daydreaming. What were you saying?"

Fred was not buying my apology, "What the hell was you looking at?"

I tried to avoid an argument and repeated that I was just daydreaming.

"Don't lie to me!"

"I'm not lying," I pleaded. "I really wasn't doing anything."

"Don't ever lie to me," he spat out again, this time violently hitting me with a crushing backhand blow to the face.

I immediately began to cry. Fred had been so nice to me. Why all of a sudden would he not believe me and think that he needed to hit me?

He stared intently into my eyes. I was fearful and confused. His voice was threatening, "Don't ever lie to me again, I mean it".

I cried harder than I had for some time. Fred's behavior left me confused and wanting to run. I could neither look at him nor speak to him. When I managed to stop crying, complete silence filled the car. I sat motionless for a long time.

Fred was the first one to speak, "What's wrong?"

I remained silent. How could he ask such a question? He had just hit me for no reason. He was overreacting and being jealous for absolutely no reason. I was the one who just been hit across the face. It still stung.

"Why are you so quiet?" He paused as if he thought I was going to answer. "I don't know what's wrong with me," I could see him forcing tears to well up in his eyes. "Sometimes I get so jealous and I am afraid that you might leave me. I don't want to lose you."

I was so invested in Fred's nonsense already. I barely knew him but he could turn things completely around so that I started to feel sorry for him. Instead I should have been demanding that he apologize for hitting me. I really believed that I was the cause for hurting him and putting our relationship at risk.

"You don't have to be jealous about anything because I love you." The deal was sealed. I had given in to Fred and now was offering him comfort for battering me. I felt powerless again just like I had before I met him.

Once Fred realized he had me where he wanted, he started the conversation about going to his house again. "You know I have a purple light in my room. Don't you want to see it?"

I did not feel like saying anything. I remained quiet.

"You're so beautiful and I want to make love to you. You know the way people do when they are in love." I am sure he thought I would give in.

I still had no intentions on having sex with Fred. I really did like being with him up until now, but I was not ready to lose my virginity. My heart raced anyway, and I thought I was in love with Fred. I had not lost sight of my Christian values but this was tearing me apart. I really did fear being punished by God if I gave in to my boyfriend. It went against everything I had been taught. I was just not ready to sleep with Fred or anyone else. All I had heard from the girls around me was useless. Maybe, I could pretend like I was experienced but still have a convincing excuse for why I would not sleep with him? I did not know how to pretend that I was not a virgin.

Fred was going to continue to press me until we had sex. He asked me directly this time. "Are you a virgin?"

I was speechless. Why was I feeling ashamed for what was really true? I hadn't been with anyone. I was only 14 and Fred was my first anything. Reluctantly and very softly I said, "No. I haven't...." I could feel his disapproval.

Fred then made a sudden move towards me. "Come on, I will do it good," he said.

I tried to convince him that my body was immature; that he would not find any pleasure in being with me. The more I protested the more he pressured me. What had I done? I guess I had led him on by trying to be something I was not. I wasn't ready to have sex and I wasn't ready to be Fred's girlfriend, either. I prayed to myself that he would let this go. "Please believe me now," I thought to myself.

He argued that I had nothing to be ashamed of. He kissed my neck and face. I felt sick and weak but there was nothing I could do. Fred's hand went between my legs, and I tried to push him away. He was on a mission and things had progressed too far. I knew I could not handle this. My boyfriend was bound and determined to have sex with me. I was far too small to fight his advances, but I still tried to resist.

Fred got visibly angry but did not raise his voice. He spoke slowly but firmly, "Stop being spoiled, or I'm not going to love you anymore." I did not respond so he tried again, "You know I can't do this if you don't want me to." He paused, "I was just playing with you anyway." Fred leaned over and gave me a hug. Maybe I had resisted just enough to get myself out of this jam.

Fred spent the rest of that day trying to convince me that I was making the wrong assumptions about him. He did love me and everything had just gotten out of hand. He tried to tell jokes to put me at ease. He tried to tell me that he hadn't really been angry with me at all. I started to think that he really did understand me and stopped because he respected my desire not to have sex right now. I even felt comfortable enough to kiss him passionately. I had been doing that for a while, so I didn't realize how that was sending mixed signals to a man who was obviously manipulating me. Having handled this crisis, I thought I was ready to handle anything in our relationship. Nevertheless, Fred still had every intention of having sex with me. He would have to wait for a better opportunity.

Some weeks passed and I started to let my guard down again. Fred asked me to ride with him to his mother's house. I did not hesitate. We had patched things up, and I had forgiven myself for causing problems in the relationship. I was still innocent. I really wanted to believe Fred could love me no matter what the circumstances were. I had denied him sex, but he was okay with that. At least that's what he said.

As soon as we arrived at the house I realized that his mother was not there. Fred had been exceedingly nice to me during the entire drive. He paid special attention to me after we walked into the house. He brought me a drink, and we sat on the couch. He put his arm around me, and we kissed. I had kissed him many times but never alone in a house.

I started thinking about the incident in his car. I wondered if he was thinking about it too. It had caused so much strain. I rejected him when he said he wanted to make love to me. I started to feel weak and afraid, looking for words that would get me out of having sex with him. It was easier before because we were in the car and very public. This time we were alone, and it would not be so easy. I thought maybe we could play sort of a game. I could let him get close, touch me a little more than he had before, but then push him away and still be in control. He told me when we had the incident in the car that he respected me, and I would not have to do anything until I wanted to. Playing my game would allow Fred to still desire me, and I would not have to completely give in.

My plan backfired. He began to grab me and handle me roughly, calling me a tease and claiming I was lying about being a virgin. "Why? Why?" he asked repeatedly.

He pressed his body hard against me with all of his weight on me so that I could not move. I asked him to stop.

"You know you want me, girl," he said. "You know it's going to be good too. Don't you?"

"No, stop," I pushed back, unable to control him.

Fred pushed down with his chest and managed to pull my shorts down from my waist. My bottom half was naked and my legs forced apart. He thrust his penis so hard that the pain felt as though my stomach was being ripped out through my vagina. He shoved even harder now that he had a firm grasp on my legs. He pulled them onto his shoulders for more leverage and when I thought it couldn't hurt anymore he began to thrust at a harder and faster pace. The more I begged and cried for him to stop the more he was determined to inflict pain on me.

"You like for me to go up in your guts?" he laughed. "I'm going to smear your blood on the walls so my boys can see it".

He laughed at me the more I screamed.

I don't know how long it lasted, but it seemed like an eternity because it has had an effect on me since then. When it was finally over, he didn't try to offer any comfort. My first instinct was to reach between my legs where I felt a wet, sticky mess. The pain was excruciating. When I pulled my hand away to see what it was and I realized that it was my own blood, I felt sick and started to cry again.

"I love the hell out of you, girl," Fred said to me. He was so happy with himself and what he had done.

What he had done to me did not feel like love at all. This hurt. This was far worse than the slap across my face. Worse than the fight with my sister. Worse than the leather belt across my back. Worse than seeing my mother in the psych ward. Worse than being poor because of my father's accident. Fred had managed to damage me more than I had already been.

I lost most virginity to someone who took advantage of me—the first man who had gained my trust, someone whom I loved unconditionally. Fred showed his love by taking from me. Taking everything he possibly could in one moment of selfishness. He took my trust, dignity, innocence, and the strength I would need to stand on my own without him. This was not going to be easily undone if it ever could be.

I believe that losing my virginity opened the floodgates to years of more abuse and self-destructive behavior. On the one hand, Fred said he loved me. I had nothing else to go on but his word, so I accepted that what he had done was normal and I should expect this every time expressed our love for each other. How sick does a person have to be to do this to a child? Because that was what I was. Despite how I felt, physically and mentally, I was in this for the long haul.

He took me home that night. I had mixed emotions about what happened. Nothing felt right about it yet I did not see any choice but to wait for my boyfriend to make love to me again.

A few days later the phone rang, as I was getting ready for school. I was going to be late again if I answered it. I quickly grabbed my books and headed for the door to meet my father. Suddenly, I stopped and decided to pick up the receiver. It was Fred's voice on the other end. I didn't want to talk to him. He promised that he loved me and what he had done to me was okay. I was too inexperienced to realize he had raped me. I was terrified and could never tell anyone.

"I have to hurry. I'm late for school," I said annoyed that he was still trying to talk to me after what had happened at his mother's house.

"Meet me outside the school," he said as if he was already there waiting for me. His voice was confident. He knew I would meet him no matter what had happened. Just hearing his voice made me reconsider being angry with him. Fred was right even after everything that had happened. I agreed to see him when my father dropped me off.

As I got into the car with my father, I slipped into one of my daydreams. I tried to imagine what kind of mood he would be in when I saw him. Maybe he missed me and would be happy to see me. His tone during our brief conversation was the one he used when he wanted to treat me nicely. Frankly, I missed him. There still was not enough abuse to make me go away. He was not going to be unpleasant. I imagined that he would not yell at me or hit me in the school parking lot.

As soon as my dad pulled in front of the school, my sister seemed to jump out of the car before it came to a complete stop. She was never going to be late if she could help it. Out of the corner of my eye, I could see Fred's car parked a few spots down from where my father had pulled in. I carefully gathered my books and said my goodbye. I walked slowly in the direction of Fred's car to give my father time to leave the parking lot. As I saw the family car disappear around the corner, my pace quickened and I approached Fred.

I was late for school again. Any more time spent with Fred was going to make me even later. Nevertheless, he got out of the car and opened the door for me like he always did. I was afraid to turn down his invitation to get in.

It was awkward at first, and I knew I had to set the right tone. I chose my words carefully. I needed to say something that would show to Fred that I wasn't rejecting him. I had been trained already without realizing it. "I missed you." I needed to stroke him. "I can tell that you missed me too."

"Yeah, it's been three days since I've seen you," he responded, not showing any hostility.

It was now safe to tell him that I had to go. "I can't miss school, Fred." The love of my life had managed to turn my brief academic success completely around. I was failing and I was on the verge of being expelled because Fred had taken me from school a lot during the grading period. I decided to keep explaining. "I have a test today, and it's very important that I do well."

"What time?" He didn't believe me.

"Third period," I responded quickly.

Before I could get out of the car he said, "Don't worry, I'll have you back in time." Fred pulled from the parking space, and we were on the road headed for goodness only knows where.

As I sat there I thought about how Fred had often encouraged me to skip school. He was not pushing me to do my schoolwork, either. He seemed to be happiest if I didn't mention school or think about anything other than being with him. However, I needed to make sure he wasn't angry because I told him I needed to take that test. "What do you want to do?" I said, partly to reassure him and also to figure out where he might be taking me.

"I have to go home. To my house and take care of some business," he said. We were headed back to Creedmoor and his mother's house. The place where he had just hurt me so bad, and I couldn't do anything to stop it.

Things started to spin out of control at home while I had been seeing Fred. The initial calm immediately after I met Fred had gone and life had reverted back to the way it had been. In hindsight, it was actually much worse because my behavior was completely out of whack. For as much as I felt like my family was mistreating me, I was only adding fuel to the fire by skipping school and letting Fred stay in my life. I missed school more than I should.

On that trip to his house, Fred did not ravage me. This was about trying to convince me to forgive him. He had to work on me to get me to consider leaving my family. I had to be willing to buy into his promises that he would make things better. He treated me better than he ever had. I was now full invested in his plan to separate me from family.

Several weeks passed and one Friday, as I arrived home from school, I made the decision that I was going to leave and never return again. The only place for me to go would be Fred's house. I wanted to be with him forever. I called him up and told him to come get me. I slipped out of the house and was gone just like that.

I do not remember much about the ride to Fred's house. I was just glad to be away from home. I do remember Fred telling me that his mother was in the hospital, and we would have the house all to ourselves. I had met his mother before. She was a sickly woman and had no control over Fred, who ran the house the way he saw fit. I remember overhearing her ask Fred how old was I. She told him that he was wrong for bringing a "baby" in her house and doing what he was doing to me. He obviously did not give a thought to what his mother thought. Everything was about him and he was not going to listen to anything she had to say about me.

When we got there, he told me that I could help him run his business. I would stay there while he ran the street operation. You can guess what kind of business he was running. How could I be so oblivious to the fact that what was going on was completely illegal? It didn't matter because I was going to be able to have nice things that the money Fred made could buy.

I did not like the idea of being in the house alone with strange men because there was a steady stream of customers that came by. I started to meet his friends, but I knew he had not stopped being jealous so I kept my distance from anyone who came by. Although I had settled into my new home, three weeks after I had been there things were about to come crashing down again.

Fred received a phone call and shortly afterwards three of his acquaintances arrived. When he met Sam, Lamont, and Terry at the front door a brief argument ensued. They wanted to come in the house but Fred suggested they stay outside.

I could hear Sam over everyone else. "Fred don't want us to come in because he doesn't want us to see the little bitch he got up in there!"

Lamont chimed in, "I ain't stud'n that girl!"

Fred eventually let the three of them in and they came into the living room where I was already seated. I was on a large sectional couch and the three positioned themselves there as well. Fred made a little small talk and then left the room to head upstairs to retrieve something. While Fred was gone, the three talked among themselves about me. I just sat there not wanting to cause any trouble.

When Fred returned, Lamont pulled out a plastic bag with what appeared to be cigars. I had been around long enough to know what kind of business Fred ran—these were not the ordinary cigars. Lamont called them baseball bats and they were the biggest he had ever seen. We all started smoking the extra large joints while we watched music videos on television. I had gone on one step further away from the values I had been taught at home. To be sitting in a room full of people who had no regard for the law and participated in the sale of illegal drugs would have horrified my mother.

We all sat there for some time doing absolutely nothing useful and yet nothing seemed unusual. Then all of a sudden Fred asked me to come upstairs with him. We left the three guests downstairs as I followed closely behind him. Fred made a path to his bedroom. In a flash he grabbed me around the neck and pulled me close to him. He told me he wanted to have sex right then, but I protested. There were people in the house, and I didn't think it was right. Fred pushed me forcefully on to the bed and slapped me hard across the face. My first instinct was to scream and I did.

I continued to wrestle with Fred and cry out loud. The sounds of our struggle caused Sam to bolt up the stairs to find out what was going on. Fred hit me again as Sam entered the room.

Sam tried to intervene on my behalf, "Fred, why you hitting that girl?"

Fred laughed, "Mind your own business and go back downstairs."

Sam complied immediately. Fred got off me and went to close the door. "Just wait until they leave," Fred said menacingly. "When I go up in you, you will know it. Cause I'm going to try and go all the way up in your guts."

He calmly opened the door and strode back down stairs as if nothing happened. I followed him not knowing what else to do.

"Man, that's fucked up," Sam offered as we reentered the living room. "Why did you have to hit that girl?"

Fred denied hitting me to Lamont and Terry. The tension in the room continued to mount as Terry teased Fred. He then suggested that he had some drugs that Fred wanted, but he wouldn't give them up. Fred was fed up with our company and told them to leave. Sam seemed the most upset about being asked to leave. As the three left, one of them suggested that if they came back it might be with pistols since Fred was going to be an inhospitable host.

As soon as the front door was closed, Fred turned to me. The look in his eyes made it clear that he was angry with me. "Are you ready for your beating?"

I dutifully marched up the steps and stripped down completely nude. Fred barely gave me time to finish taking my clothes off before he set upon me. He pushed me down on the bed. This time he didn't slap me. He grabbed both of my legs behind the knees and hoisted them high into the air. The insides of my knees rested on his shoulders giving him the maximum leverage to punish me again. I braced my non-lubricated self. Fred never hesitated. Every thrust was deep and vicious. He had promised that it would get better each time he "made love to me" but this hurt worse than the first time. He pounded harder and harder, the more he sensed I was hurting.

When Fred ejaculated, he was finished. He never once tried to pleasure me in the way he explained in that first phone conversation. When he got up, I could see blood everywhere. The sheets were covered as well as my inner thighs. Had I waited for God to give me this?

Fred tried to comfort me using only the logic he could use. He said that this was what happened to everyone who was with him. They all bled because his penis was so big. What happened to me was normal, and I needed to get used to it.

I wish I had known then that his story was just his twisted way of controlling me. I was giving him everything I had of me. I showed Fred nothing but love, but the only thing I got in return was a terrible pounding whenever he felt like it. He kept telling me he loved me and that he cared. For the time being I would have to let this pass. I could not just pick up the phone and call home.

Terry, Lamont, and Sam returned later on in the evening. I suppose they had patched up whatever differences they had with Fred. I was sitting on the couch again when they came in. There was no confrontation at the door like before. They sat either side of me and tried to strike up a conversation. I didn't say anything. I was still terrified for the punishment I had received. Apparently, I deserved what I had gotten because I had sent signals that I might be interested in any or all of the guests.

Lamont seemed to be the provocateur this time. He sat near me and looked me over from head-to-toe in a provocative manner. He meant to cause some trouble. Talking to Fred, he said, "Oh, my fault, I forgot this is your girl."

Terry moved his hand to the spot on the couch behind me, and I arched my back to avoid his touch. Lamont watched him closely and they both chuckled as I tried not to call any attention to what they were doing.

"What are they laughing about," asked Fred?

I dared not say anything. I was sure he would blame me for being flirtatious instead of them for being too forward. They began to talk about their past and their many sexual exploits. I kept silent. Out of the blue, Fred told them I was cheating on him. I didn't confirm or deny his allegations because it would only provoke a confrontation. Even so, there was no way that could be true. I was trapped in Fred's mother's house in Creedmoor. It was just Fred's sick delusion and obsessive jealous streak that made him fear me being with someone else. I was too brainwashed to know how to take the first steps to get out of the situation.

The three expressed their disbelief that I was doing anything behind Fred's back. They talked about me openly as if I wasn't there. They commented on my body without regard to how it would make me feel. I felt like a piece of meat.

"Would you turn her down if you had a chance?" Fred asked.

"Hell, yeah," Sam said. I suppose he was thinking about how jealous Fred acted over me.

Just then one of my favorite songs was playing in the background. Fred got the idea that I should dance to the song and entertain our guests. I had been so thoroughly indoctrinated with Fred's sick view of the world that I didn't mind dancing. I liked it and since being with Fred, I had danced for his friends before. They would throw money at me while I performed, and it gave me my own money to put away. It didn't occur to me that it was exploitative for a 14-year-old girl to be dancing for grown men, but they wanted to see me perform.

As I gyrated to the music, they all seemed to be getting excited. Fred joined in the conversation. Our three guests wondered aloud what it was like to have sex with me. I heard every word of their conversation but never thought they meant it. Fred would never let another man touch me. He had told me often that I was not to even think about being with another man, or it would cost me dearly.

When the music finished, Fred suggested that I go up to the bedroom with him. I declined. I was still sore from earlier in the day, and I didn't want to go through that again. Not a wise decision on my part. Fred slapped me again but this time he did not care if anyone saw what he did. He demanded that I go up to the bedroom. I dutifully consented.

When we got up to the bedroom, Fred just yelled at me, telling me not to embarrass him in front of his friends ever again. He sat me down on the bed and told me not to move. Suddenly he left without a word.

To my surprise, Terry entered the room, sat down beside me, and began to touch me as if we were alone. I thought Terry must have gone completely crazy. He must have known that he was putting my life and his life in danger. If Fred found out I would get the worst beating of my life. I couldn't scream to call attention to what was happening so I just sat there.

In no time Terry managed to pull up my shirt. I didn't resist. Now he was kissing and sucking my breast. His hand reached beneath my skirt and moved towards my vagina. I was terrified. I tried to whisper as quietly as I could to warn Terry to stop, but he kept going.

"Be quiet or Fred might find out," Terry told me.

Lamont entered the room as Terry continued to fondle me. He spoke loudly as if to draw attention, "Terry, what are you doing?"

Terry didn't answer. He kept touching me all over and sucking my breast. Lamont joined him on the bed sitting on the opposite side. Lamont reached under my skirt and pulled my panties off.

They both laid me back on the bed and I was still too frightened to protest. Terry removed his pants and started to penetrate me. Fred walked in the room. Lamont and Terry stopped for a moment as Fred walked towards us. Fred was smiling and laughing.

Terry moved out of the way as Fred came closer. Fred drew back and hit me hard against my face. It wasn't a slap this time. He punched me and sent me reeling.

"That's a little freak you got, Fred," Lamont said. "She likes it rough."

Fred slapped me in the face several more times. He told me to be quiet because I brought this on myself. He said that when they were talking about having sex with me earlier, I didn't object. That meant I wanted them to all take turns with me. I did not say anything earlier because I did not want to make Fred angry. Now he was angry because I did not speak up for myself. I was confused and thought that there was no way to win with Fred. Was he letting them have their way with me just because they said they wanted to? What about his being so jealous of every man that even looked at me?

Fred removed his clothes and the three of them were naked and eager to abuse me. Each one of them took their turns on top of me. All pounding at my already damaged vagina. I couldn't feel anything anymore. I just lay there and cried. I wasn't able to scream. It would not have ended the torture. Each time it appeared to end, the rape continued... for almost eight hours. When they were finally finished, my hairline was soaked from my tears. I couldn't move and I felt numb from the waist down.

"Did you think you were going to have sex with my friends and get away with it?" Fred slapped me again. "You're a nasty slut!"

I could only turn my face away. I was not going to be able to stop Fred from doing whatever he wanted to.

Lamont tried to reason with Fred, "How can you hit her? She's just a little girl."

"It's easy," Fred said. "You do it like this." Another heavy blow landed.

I touched my face, and it felt like a water balloon about to burst. My eyes were swollen and puffy and my ears felt as if they were stuffed with cotton. Every word they said was muffled. I tried to get up. I wanted to get away in case Fred wanted to hit me again. I was disoriented and rolled out of the bed onto the floor. I couldn't escape because I could not even get to my feet.

"Get up!" Fred demanded. He must have known that I was already in terrible pain from what happened. I was faced down and totally at his mercy. Fred began to kick me with heavy blows to the side. "Get up!"

I could only moan and try to tell Fred that he was killing me. Clearly I thought I was going to die there. He continued to laugh at me as I begged for mercy.

"I'm not going to sit here and watch you kill her," Lamont said. "It looks like she's dying.

Fred laughed even harder. "She'll be alright." Then he addressed me, "Cris, are you alright?" Fred got close to my face as if to check to see if I was still breathing. I could feel his breath as he watched me closely. "Don't scare me like that." He seemed to be worried that I was not responding. "We will be together forever."

I was fading out and could not stop the sensation of passing into unconsciousness. I could see everything I had done since meeting Fred pass before my eyes. Coming to be with him had been a terrible mistake.

I don't know when the three scumbags left the room. I only remember sitting in the corner with my head down and my arms covering my head. I was crying and saying, "leave me alone" again and again. I opened my eyes and realized I was already alone. The room was dark with only a tiny lamp shining on the far side. I rocked back and forth to comfort myself but rocking only made me hurt worse. Every inch of my body ached and with each movement, I could recall each thrust. I could not clear the thoughts out of my mind.

The way Fred had sex with me was pure anger that he was expressing as a result of some mental illness he had. No matter what he tried to tell me, I knew then that Fred was using me for his own sick pleasure and amusement. He was a pedophile and sadist who preyed on me, and likely on other young girls before and after my time with him. I knew the difference now between sex and making love, even if I couldn't do a thing about it.

When Fred finally came into the bedroom, I looked up at him and his expression had completely changed. His facial expressions and demeanor were foreign to the monster I had witnessed only a few hours before. My heart pounded and I could feel a single tear roll down one side of my face.

"Why are you still on the floor?" Was he serious? Did he not remember what he had just done to me? Calmly, he said, "Do you want to get up?"

I shook my head yes and Fred reached down to lift me up and place me on the bed. He left and returned with several ice packs. I jerked as he placed one on my face. The cold stung and offered more pain at first than immediate relief. He also brought me something to drink, orange juice as I recall. I sipped juice slowly. It made me throw up.

I finally stopped thinking about the attack and my mind wandered to my parents. Did they care about where I was?

Were they looking for me? For the first time since I left, I wanted to be at home.

I eventually drifted off to sleep, but it was a fitful and restless sleep. Each time I awoke, I could feel my entire body aching. My head, between my legs, my stomach, and every inch of me was bruised from the assaults.

I'm not exactly sure how long I rested but decided that I needed to get out of the bed and take a shower. The smell of the rape was still on me, and I needed to wash it away. Each time I tried to stand, I would fall back on the bed. It was difficult to get my balance at first. I kept trying until I could stand. The walk to the bathroom was an ordeal, but the shower was a great relief.

Now it was time to make my way down the stairs as I was starving. When I reached the kitchen, Fred sat at the table smoking a cigar as if he didn't have a care in the world. I didn't look at him, but walked right past him without a word. I was so angry and wanted to lash out, but I came to get something to eat.

"Cris, I'm really sorry about last night. You know, we were all high, and we want you to know that we didn't mean any of it." He paused, "Cris, are you mad? I won't let you hang with us anymore. I'm afraid you might get hurt."

"*Get* hurt?" I thought to myself. This was no accident. What did he mean? Was he trying to minimize what they had done to me?

He was trying to make this my fault like every other time he had abused me. He made it seem that he could only control himself if I would just "do better." But how was I supposed to prevent him from being provoked? He was in a constant state of provocation.

I have never stopped feeling ashamed of what happened to me. I started to pretend I was a tough girl and could take anything. Deep down, I have been too ashamed to admit the lasting impact of my time with Fred. I pushed those feelings back to the far reaches of my brain. My soul would grow dark and my heart hard at times in my attempt to deal with what happened to me. I put on a front with people for so long and never mentioned the rape. Consequently, in my effort to hide my trauma from everyone, I never allowed myself to grieve. I have found it hard to grieve about anything.

I did not bolt from the room or call for someone to come and get me immediately because I was still in love with Fred. It's so difficult to get away from someone while you are being abused. I'm sure people don't understand the dynamic. I don't fully understand it myself. You are crushed mentally as well as physically. I do think you can put things aside and move on. That is what I tried to do, forget the incident, but it is always there. Subconsciously, the gang rape continues to have a lasting effect on me. It was especially troubling back then when I had no experience in the world. It made me think that every man was like that. Worse, it made me feel like I was dirty and nasty. Not just the next day but everyday afterwards and for years. I couldn't get the sights, sounds, smells, and feelings out of my head. It permeates your entire life and determines how you interact with people and the choices you ultimately end up making.

I was a difficult person to deal with and, frankly, it was hard for me to live with myself. I internalized the blame for what had happened to me. Fred was excellent at manipulation like most abusers. Carrying the burden of the shame for being involved in this kind of trauma left me in a perpetual state of depression for years.

Fred took me back home but there was no way to be normal again. Having been introduced to a very hard and fast life and suffering from major depression set me on a course for my first encounter with the mental health system.

Still not able to tell anyone about what happened, I hit rock bottom in the second week of December 1993. My depression was debilitating and I didn't eat. I could only manage to lie in bed and cry day and night. My mother grew particularly concerned with my behavior. Perhaps she knew something had been done to me because of what had happened to her as a child.

I remember the moment when my mother made a decision to take me to Duke University Medical Center's Emergency Department. It was and still is a very sad day in my memory.

The doctors at Duke diagnosed me with Post Traumatic Stress Disorder (PTSD). They also felt the best course of treatment would be to have me institutionalized. I was placed in back of a police car for the first time and transported to John Umstead Psychiatric Hospital as if I was a criminal. I was the one who had suffered so much, but now I was being taken away.

I would be in the hospital for two months of intensive therapy and medication. I was talking to a steady stream of people all day, everyday. It did make me feel better. I felt less overwhelmed. I was instructed to end communications with Fred. Even so, I was constantly tempted to reach out to him. I had access to a phone, and I wanted to take care of the unfinished business I had with Fred. I was beginning to understand how much damage he had caused and wanted to confront him about it.

As soon as I had a chance, I called Fred and he seemed happy to hear from me. I knew my family did not want me to have anything to do with him, but I went back to seeing him clandestinely as soon as I got out of the hospital. The good feelings I was having were only short-lived as he became violent and abusive again.

Getting out the relationship with Fred this time wasn't just a matter of walking away.

When I told Fred I could not continue on with him he told me that he would rather see me dead than be with another man. Coming from Fred, that was a serious concern.

He had shown his capacity to be evil, and I believed he was capable of killing me. I regret that I ever met Fred.

Rocking the Boat

Fred continued to be a part of my life even though he had no right to. Sometimes I think he still is although he is not physically present. Some things never leave your mind. I know there is someone reading this who has a Fred in her past or present and who experienced the devastation that kind of abuse leaves on a person's soul.

Even after I was admitted for psychiatric help, I still found it difficult to break away from Fred.

I tried to have other boyfriends after Fred. Despite the dysfunctional relationship I had been in, I still longed for the attention that a boyfriend-girlfriend relationship offered. It is sad that I had no real foundation for establishing a good relationship. When I did find a boyfriend, Fred tried to undermine the relationship. He called incessantly. Fred also continued to make veiled threats, implying that I would be much safer if I was with him than without him. As I grew bolder and rejected him outright, the threat became direct and frightening. The degree of obsession and jealousy on Fred's part should be disturbing to everyone who has a daughter. Feeling lost and thrown away, girls seek the first man who can offer her something positive. Fred preyed on my vulnerability and could have easily killed me. As a consequence of Fred's obsession, I am a damaged person today.

My early dating life has had a profound and lasting negative effect on my self-esteem. Even when Fred wasn't around, I often found myself taking the blame for things I did not do and that were beyond my control. My daydreams no longer contained anything to do with being a ballerina. I was constantly asking myself, "Why me?" Moreover, I would often ask God, "Why had I met him?" I had been specific with God, but it seemed as though my answered prayer was just a cruel hoax. Constantly in the search for a reason to justify my existence, I could find none. I still wanted to be loved so badly.

Now that I was no longer a virgin, it seemed that every boy or man I encountered only wanted to have sex with me. No one wanted to get to know me. I noticed how much older—too old, in fact—men were who showed an interest in me. They were so forward about wanting to have sex with me. It was as if I had a sign around my neck saying I am available. Somehow the experience with Fred changed the way I carried myself and people could see it or feel it. I was no longer pure and a virgin and that came across.

Amid all the turmoil that was my life, I did meet a few people who were good to me. One young man, a 19-year-old, expressed an interest in dating me. He is still the closest person to my age that I have ever dated. I'm sure this says something about my personality and how the trauma of being with Fred shaped me.

Luckily, this person came along at a time when I could accept him into my life not matter what his age happened to be. This was one of the few people to touch me with his kindness and willingness to listen. Our time together provided me with some optimism that there was a hopeful future and brighter tomorrow even for me. I believe he genuinely wanted what was best for me. I felt joyful when we spent time together. I considered him to be my first real boyfriend and when he caressed me it was as if he listened to me and was trying to comfort me. I never felt pressured or coerced into sex by his gestures.

In an odd twist, I was the one who sometimes pressed for sex. Even after the trauma, I didn't know that sex did not equal love. I would be aggressive and my boyfriend would have to push me away. My boyfriend told me that he loved me, and he would do anything in the world that I asked. Our relationship was not conditioned on having sex. I had never heard such a thing but when I realized he was sincere, it did a lot to repair some of the damage I had suffered. I did not have to have sex to make him happy because he just wanted to spend time with me. That was such a departure from the past. I thought he was the nicest person in the world.

When I got to the point I was able to accept his love and concern for me, he abruptly broke up with me. I had six months of bliss, and it was gone just like that. I was so sad that day. I'm sure my parents were sad too. The good relationship had provided some protection for me against the forces that disrupted the house.

The more I was at peace the more the rest of the family was also. The sad reality is that I was dumped on account of my damaged personality. I did not know how to accept the love that was being offered to me on a silver platter. I was too immature, the damage Fred had inflicted on me caused me to be a selfish person. I learned that relationships were about manipulation and who was in control. You just took what you could and too bad about the other person's feelings. My immaturity led me to a desperate, always ineffective method to get my boyfriend back. I told him that I couldn't live without him, implying that I would kill myself if he wouldn't take me back. This was a tactic I had taken directly from Fred's relationship handbook.

I threatened that I would go back to Fred if I couldn't be with him. Undoubtedly, he would have me back with that threat because I had told him everything about Fred. That did not help either.

The night after our breakup, I decided I would follow through on my plan to kill myself. I rode to the grocery store with my father with the intent of buying some drugs that I could overdose on to end my misery. I wasn't sure what to get. When we returned home, I had a bottle of aspirin with me.

I thought again and again about why this would be the best thing for everyone.

I could hear Fred's voice ringing in my ear, "No one is going to love you but me!" That was enough to seal the deal. I wasn't going to be loved by Fred anymore. It was too painful.

Around 10:00 pm I went into the bathroom and locked the door. In multiples of six, I took all 60 aspirins in the bottle and went to bed. Of course, I did not die as planned, but when I awoke I shook violently. I saw huge a black spot in my line of vision. I felt better intermittently and even went out with my father the next morning. While riding in the car with my father and sister, the symptoms returned. My energy faded away; I grew dizzy and confused; I wanted to sleep; I felt exhausted; and I began acting irrationally, crawling, twisting, and turning along the floor of the car. My father noticed my behavior in the rear mirror and wanted to know what was the matter.

My sister offered her opinion that there was nothing wrong with me and that I was faking to draw attention.

My father asked again, "Cris, what's wrong with you?"

My speech was slurred as I tried to respond. I tried to tell him that I had taken the entire bottle of aspirin. After several attempts, I finally got it out. I could no longer hold my head still, and I shook uncontrollably. I saw the look of concern on my father's face and that served to increase my anxiety. I thought that maybe I was really going to die.

"Daddy, don't believe her," my sister insisted. "If she had taken a whole bottle of aspirin, she would be dead."

My father ignored my sister for a change. He asked, "When did you take them?"

"About 10 o'clock last night," I said.

"Well, it is 12 now. We still may have time to get to the hospital."

It had been about 14 hours since I took the 60 pills.

My sister found the incident funny. She laughed and suggested, "Maybe we can stop at Hardee's on the way to get something to eat." She was still unaware or didn't care about the severity of the situation.

We didn't stop for a sandwich. My father headed straight for Duke Medical Center and the emergency room, where the doctors pumped my stomach and sent me for testing to make certain none of my internal organs were damaged. I remember my mother being at my bedside, trying to comfort me. There were tubes coming from my nose and mouth. Telling stories about my birth and early childhood, she talked about how joyful she had been when I was a baby. I had never heard her talk like that. Perhaps my family did love me and this had given them a wake-up call. However, it was costly. I stayed in the intensive care unit for two weeks. My mental health was in shambles. I spent another two weeks in Duke's psychiatric ward.

This was the beginning of my battle with major depression. There would be many more times as I got older that I would slip in and out of major depressive episodes. This would also be my last inpatient treatment while I was still in the care of my parents. In addition to the depression, there were so many other things with which I had to deal. Chief among them was that I had developed serious trust issues and every succeeding relationship caused more problems. The more I sought love, the more wrong choices I would make.

Despite all of the challenges of being a teenager and my mental health issues, I managed to graduate from Hillside High School in 1996. I was not a dumb person. I just made dumb mistakes. Had I applied myself the entire time I could have been just like my sister.

After graduation I needed to be away from Durham and part of that plan was to join the military. I felt stable and able to control myself emotionally for a change. I met and married my first husband Kenneth. He was 14 years my senior. I was back to my pattern of being with much older men. I had been through so much already that I did not think anyone my age would be able to understand me. The one time I had tried, I ran that person away.

There were other good reasons *not* to be with Kenneth. Like Fred, he had jealousy issues. He also had limitations in his ability to support us. He was unable to read or write. That posed a serious economic challenge for us. That meant I was not able to go to college at that juncture.

Joining the Navy would allow me to take care of a multitude of issues. I could be away from Durham, my husband could go along, we would not have to hear from my family about their concerns, and we would have housing and other benefits that would lessen some of the financial pressures.

Basic training at Great Lakes was my first post. I was eventually stationed in Virginia Beach where my husband could join me. During that time I started to teach my husband to read and write. He made great progress. Kenneth was eventually able to complete his own job application. After Virginia Beach, we headed to California with much hope and many dreams. I fully expected to stay in the Navy for my entire commitment but that was unfortunately not going to happen.

At first, my husband seemed to be caring and attentive. Consequently, I started off with a great deal of hope and never looked at this as a short-term situation. I thought I was going to help him improve his situation and things for me could only get better. I still possessed one fatal shortcoming: I was a terrible judge of character. I also still looked for a man to dominate and be jealous over me. It was not a conscious decision to get into another such relationship. I looked at it in terms of degrees. Kenneth was no saint either, just much better than what I had known. Being kindhearted and a caring person is a character flaw that I suffer from. I was more concerned about Kenneth than myself.

My military career was good. For the first time in my life, I was in control of my destiny. I now had a good group of friends and co-workers who like me were trying to improve their lives. I was also seeing places for the first time like Hollywood, Los Angeles, and San Diego. In the Navy, my peers were not only my age but shared the same struggles. I found women aboard ship with whom I could talk. I also found socialization with shipmates, but unfortunately I developed a taste for alcohol. Our gatherings included a lot of heavy drinking.

The breakup with my husband was inevitable. We were very different after all. The age difference was a significant factor but there was always the potential for an explosion residing near the surface. It would be fueled by my husband's jealousy and, I believe, his insecurity. When I decided to leave him our appearance was seen as a normal relationship. The truth was that this marriage was chaotic. I was accustomed to being in constant conflict with my partner. There was always a chance that this marriage would come apart, and it did.

Kenneth's cousin and wife lived in the same military housing, less than five minutes way. Little did I know that one of my neighbors was a good friend of the cousin's wife. The nosy neighbor watched me obsessively and reported back to my husband that she saw the cousin often coming and going from our house, and that we must be having an affair.

Kenneth's jealousy boiled over one Friday night when we were all playing cards. We had been playing for a spell when Kenneth decided he needed a cigarette break and excused himself from the table. While he was outside, his cousin jokingly suggested that we peep at Kenneth's cards. "Let's cheat," he said as he elbowed me and laughed with a wink.

Kenneth could not bare the thought of anyone showing me any attention. He chose to believe there was evidence of me cheating. He was waiting for the opportunity to catch me. Despite the innocent nature of the jesting between his cousin and me, it was enough for Kenneth to prove that I was up to no good.

He bolted quickly into the house. "Cris," he looked agitated, "may I talk to you outside?"

I got up from the table, and we stood outside silently for a moment. Without a word, Kenneth slapped me across the face. Stumbling, I was sent reeling to the ground. I had learned from the abuse Fred dished out that it was safer if I didn't fight back. If I tried to stay calm, it would de-escalate the situation quicker. Without saying a word, I struggled to regain my composure.

Kenneth finally had to say something. "Didn't I tell you that I see everything? I want you to know that I saw everything you did in there. Why were you flirting with my cousin?"

"I thought you were better than that," he went on.

That was it. If my husband would hit me over this, he would continue to hit me. The interchange with his cousin was so innocuous that I couldn't begin to imagine how I would be able to have any contact with any males. Here in the Navy there were men everywhere and I spent weeks at a time at sea with males. What would he think if he saw what life aboard the ship was like?

Right then was the time to free myself from further years of misery. It took me a long time to be rid of Fred. I was getting older and I saw that other women were independent. In this marriage I was the one with a career and skills. My husband depended on me for what he had.

Kenneth had been verbally abusing and threatening me already, but I took that. Now that he had crossed into physical abuse, I could not take any more cruelty. As I lay there I thought about how he was controlling what I wore when I was out of uniform. He also didn't allow me to offer any opinion or idea about anything. Conversations we had were always one-sided, always about whatever he wanted to talk about. Worse still was the fact that he did not mind embarrassing me in public. I made up my mind that this was the last night I was going to be with him. I was going to move back to the USS Mount Hood where I was assigned. I was resolute in my decision, and I felt good about it. I would be free from constant watching and could move around freely.

Aboard the ship I did feel free. I even felt like it was okay to have male friendships. That is how I met Ryan. We became fast friends and were inseparable. I had no thought that we would go beyond being friends. He was suddenly someone in my life who would do things I dreamt about. He is the one who took me to Hollywood, Disneyland, Universal Studios, and museums in the Los Angeles area. We had late night dinners in cool restaurants or would go down to the dock and sit and talk for hours. Our long conversations were always refreshing. I was even warming up to the notion that we could be in a long-term relationship. I did not see a future with Kenneth.

In one aspect Ryan and I were very different. I was black and he was white. I never dated a white man. He treated me well and that's all that mattered. I was not one to deliberate about whether getting into a relationship was a good idea or a bad one. Ryan treated me better than I had been treated by anyone else. Of course, there was one problem with moving ahead with my new love: I was still married.

Rumors spread fast in military communities and my nosy former neighbor somehow got the word that I was seeing Ryan. She dutifully reported what she knew to my husband. Determined to cause me the maximum amount of trouble, Kenneth promptly called the captain of the ship to report my affair at 3 am.

I was caught off guard when the captain approached me about my illicit relationship. He was friendly and calmly told me, "Your husband has been calling the ship and complaining about your affair with Ryan. I would not have bothered you if not for the fact that he was calling at 3:00 am every morning." He went on, "The last phone call was very troubling and, as you know, you have already been to captain's mast (disciplinary action) for a separate incident. I cannot continue to receive any more threats from him. You must do something or we will have to let you go".

It was agreed that my husband and I would meet to settle our differences. The meeting took place in the chaplain's office. My husband, the captain and I would be able to have the chaplain settle our dispute quietly. Of course the meeting did not go so well. Within a few minutes total chaos ensued and the entire ship erupted into a frenzy.

Honk! Honk! The ship's horn was sounded. "Security alert! Security alert! All hands on deck, port and starboard! An intruder is aboard! Location P32! Chaplain's office!" The warning went out over the loudspeakers aboard the Mt. Hood. The announcer continued with more instructions on safety procedures. The scene in the chaplain's office was total disarray.

"I just want my wife," Kenneth was screaming.

He lunged towards me so quickly I could feel the breeze caused by his sudden move towards me. He was determined to take me back with him or harm me in front of everyone. He was so committed to getting at me that it took four men to subdue him. The more the Shore Patrol tried to hold him back, the more he clawed his way towards me. They were trying to drag him in the opposite direction. It looked like one pile of football players coming in my direction.

I jumped from my seat and ran for the safest place I could find in the room. I cowered in the corner crying. It shook me to think that he would attempt to board the ship with hundreds of armed men and still attempt to hurt me. When he was finally wrestled to the ground, the guards quickly escorted me back to my living quarters. I curled up in my small bunk and cried myself to sleep.

When I returned to the galley to work, I was bombarded with questions from my crewmates. My husband's antics had caused a stir and the news got around the ship. I wanted Kenneth out of my life and to be with Ryan. However, it would not be that easy because Kenneth would not give up so easily. He soon embarked on his plan to make me pay.

Before I cleared up my mess with Kenneth, I began a sexual relationship with Ryan. Our liaisons provided comfort for me but also resulted in my becoming pregnant with my first child. When we confirmed that I was pregnant, he did not hesitate in expressing his desire to be with me and raise our child together as a family.

I remember the night very well. We met at the Laundromat at the end of the pier. It was one of the places we could see each other away from the ship. It was nighttime. This was a completely different relationship in so many ways, but now I was carrying my lover's child. All of the previous sex never led to a pregnancy. I felt so passionately in love with my new man.

Ryan's eyes were the bluest I had ever seen. He looked at me impassionedly, "I love you more than anything. I want to be with you the rest of my life, and I want you to be my wife." He went on, "No matter what we go through in our life, we'll do it together."

I cried in Ryan's arms that night. I think he cried too. We were both overjoyed. There was another life involved, and I needed to make sure that this did not turn out like every other relationship. I believed with all of my heart that this was the right thing to do. I was going to have this baby. One problem was the Navy had a say in my personal life.

My husband returned to North Carolina but immediately began contacting my captain. This time he complained that I refused to reimburse him for the cost of relocating back home. My refusal to pay for his plane ticket caused even more problems for me with the leadership team on the ship.

"He's your spouse," explained the captain, "and therefore it's your responsibility that you take care of him."

"My responsibility?" I thought.

Kenneth tried to kill me in front of the chaplain and the captain, and I was required to be responsible for him. It made me angry. He had tried to destroy my car, my possessions, and had left me in debt before he departed, which I tried to explain to the captain. I had been trying to repair the damage to our military home that he left in shambles. That was in addition to $10,000 in bills and a wrecked car. None of that impressed the Navy. The decision was made that I must assume all responsibility for the damages, the debt, and Kenneth.

I understood their logic but I didn't want to accept it. Kenneth would not have been in California had I not made a commitment to join the Navy in the first place. Nevertheless, I was bound and determined to remain resolute and not change my thinking based on what I considered to be the right thing. I refused to give him anything. My decision to provoke a standoff was not the wisest move I could have made. It led to a disciplinary hearing concerning the issue.

The "captain's mast" is the Navy's way of handling discipline problems with sailors short of a court martial. They call it non-judicial punishment because you are not convicted of a crime, but it adversely affects your military record. I was going to hold my ground and try to give my side of the story again. I had to appear before the captain, and I was ordered to pay for my husband's relocation expenses. I was additionally warned to stay away from Ryan and end our relationship. Both judgments were within the regulations of the Navy, but I told myself that I was going to stand on principle. I made up my mind that I was not going to do either—pay relocation expenses for Kenneth or end the relationship with Ryan.

Ryan was kind to me and was soon to be the father of my first-born. We resorted to sneaking around to see each other. We were eventually caught and I was in deep trouble again. I was called before the "captain's mast" again. This time I was not only warned but restricted to quarters. I could not leave the ship and was only allowed to do my job for two weeks.

Ryan and I were desperate to see each other, and we did everything we could to maintain our relationship. Carelessly, we were caught for a second time and there was no third "captain's mast." They were fed up and I was asked to leave the ship. I was given a general discharge from the Navy. Being almost two-months pregnant with Ryan's child, I tried to remain optimistic. Ryan promised me that we would be together as a family very soon.

Fortunately, I continued to receive benefits for six months after my discharge, which allowed me to prepare for our expected child. Ryan was sending me money. I was able to get a job at Taco Bell for three months before I had to go on bed rest.

It had been tough going through most of my pregnancy alone. I wanted so badly to be with Ryan, but I waited patiently because there would be a time when Ryan and I would live together with our child. When I had my son, I was overcome with joy but was sad as well. The first year of my son's life I was afraid to let him out of my sight. He was all I had and I did not want to lose him. My divorce was final in May of 1999.

The three of us headed for Bremerton, Washington, where Ryan had been assigned. We found a small one-bedroom apartment on his military pay. I found a job and Ryan continued his military obligation. We seemed to be building a happy little nest. Unexpectedly, I became pregnant again shortly after settling down in Washington. I was ecstatic at the prospect of adding to the family. Ryan was anything but happy. I was disappointed and upset that he didn't see it the way I did. Having another baby would stretch us financially but bind us closer together. At least that is what I hoped. Ryan did not see it that way because he was afraid we would have to struggle even harder, and that was not something he wanted to do.

I was happy and madly in love with Ryan and did not care about the finances. Being a military spouse was not suitable for me. Living where we did in Washington was depressing because of all the rain. The strain started to build between the two of us. I thought it would be best if I went back to North Carolina until things changed. Maybe some time away would make Ryan see that things were going to be okay.

It was difficult leaving Ryan. Ryan had every right to worry about how to make ends meet with two small children. I wasn't thinking rationally at all. I had grandiose illusions that things would just take care of themselves. It was much harder than I could ever imagine returning to North Carolina. Raising small children is expensive and funds were going to be very tight for a long time.

My beautiful daughter came into the world on April 12, 2000. Again I was overjoyed and thought this was the best thing that could have happened to me. Ryan made the trip to be at the hospital when she was born. I thought that maybe this meant that we would be a real family. He was here, and he seemed to be happy to be involved.

Ryan's visit turned out to be just that—a visit. He stayed with us for a week and was gone again. I cherished the time he did spend with us. He was so considerate and seemed more so than ever.

I truly loved my little gifts from God and no matter what Ryan decided to do I would have to take care of them. When he left Durham that would be the end of our relationship. We drifted apart and he eventually married someone else. I would go looking for someone else to fill the void he left. I seemed to be in constant need of a companion. I was especially needy right now as I needed help raising two small kids on my own.

My daughter Anna was four-months-old and my son, RJ as he was nick-named, was eighteen months when I decided to start another relationship. I know it wasn't long after I had been so madly in love with Ryan, but I knew he wasn't coming back. I needed to move on. I fell back to my formula. My new man was a street-smart guy named Eric.

Eric was nothing like Ryan. He was a car salesman and good at what he did. I found a job at a car dealership in Durham and we worked together there, which led to our romance. Eric came across as intelligent, but I had to learn the hard way that he had serious issues. My relationship with Eric lasted nine months. It came to a crashing halt when he seriously betrayed my trust by putting one of my most precious gifts, my son RJ, at risk.

I had to rush RJ to the hospital. Eric was the cause, which I didn't know at the time.

I normally picked Anna and RJ up at midnight after getting off my second-shift job. I worked at Nortel Networks in Research Triangle Park (RTP) and towards the end of my shift, I called my aunt to let her know I was on the way to pick the kids up as usual. My aunt informed me that Eric had uncharacteristically picked them up earlier in the day. That was not usual in the least but I let it go, figuring there must have been a good reason for him to get them early. I decided not to worry and waited for Eric to come pick me up from work.

When Eric arrived, I was completely exhausted. It did not strike me as odd that RJ was sluggish because it was late. As we drove to my parents' house and talked about the events of the day, Eric mentioned that RJ had broken one of his mother's expensive lamps and she was upset about it. I was later to learn that the story was not true and that he had not taken the children to his mother's house.

We finally arrived at my parents' and as I went to get RJ and Anna from the car it was clear that something was wrong with my son. RJ was unable to stand up on his own, and he refused to walk. Eric then insisted that he be carried into the house. Offering to carry RJ into the house was also unusual behavior for Eric. He had often complained that RJ acted like a baby, and I should not be carrying him. He was always telling me that RJ was big enough to walk on his own, and now he was the one being soft on him.

It was after midnight, so I needed to be as quiet and not disturb anyone else who was sleeping. It was dark and I didn't turn on any of the lights as we made our way to the bedroom. I put the children down and slipped into my own sleeping clothes first. Now that I was ready to crash from exhaustion, I still had to dress the kids. I reached for RJ and he moaned whenever I touched him anywhere. I just wanted to go to sleep but something wasn't right as my son began to cry.

As I turned on the light I could see that my dear son was completely covered in bruises. I screamed uncontrollably. My first thought was, "This is how my parents must have felt when I came home from being with Fred." More upsetting than the shock of seeing the bruises was the terrible fear that I might lose my son.

As I rushed RJ to the emergency room, I wondered what Eric had been doing to him all those times I left him alone with RJ. I tortured myself thinking how I had left my son alone with a monster that would hurt him so badly.

I remembered one particular time vividly. I heard RJ's cries as Eric spanked him for crying while he got a bath. I had left Eric to bathe RJ, trusting that he was teaching him how to clean himself. God only knows what else he was doing to him.

I would receive another punch to my stomach when the emergency room doctor notified me that they additionally suspected that my baby had been sexually abused. How could Eric do this to my baby? My mind ran through the whole range of emotions from shock to blaming myself and asking what could I have done to prevent this from happening. I was really angry and wanted to kill the person who would harm my child.

After we left the emergency room and I got RJ situated at home, I had to deal with my anger. I rushed to Eric's house and banged on his door. As I banged and screamed for Eric to come out, the only thing on my mind was my son's bruised body. I was even more angry when I thought about how Eric may have violated him. It was not enough that RJ was beaten to where he couldn't walk; Eric had also tried to intimidate RJ into not telling what happened. Eric even had the nerve to come to the emergency room and asked to see RJ as he was being treated.

I also thought about all the times that Eric told me that RJ was a bad child. He told me that I wanted to be around my son too much, and he needed to be with a man to learn some discipline. He had spanked RJ before, and every time he did he would take him into the bathroom and not allow me to watch.

Had he been sexually molesting my son then too? Was he doing it right under my nose in the guise of disciplining him? I thought that I must be a horrible parent. I had received spankings as a child and thought it was a normal part of bringing up children but this was something totally different. He was using my son as a sexual object. My mother, me, and now my son were part of a long chain of sexual abuse.

I had left Eric alone with both of my children countless times. There were times when I was so tired from work and he agreed to watch them for me. Many times he would take them into a room and close the door because he said he "didn't want to disturb me." Now I thought, "Was Eric doing something to Anna too?" It was unbearable. I was filled with rage and could have killed if I could only get my hands on him.

I vowed that never again would I leave my children exposed like that. No man or relationship was worth the long-term damage that physical and sexual abuse could lead to. I was a perfect example. My life was completely upset again on account of a man and a bad decision to pursue a relationship. I was racked with guilt that I might be setting up my own children for failure.

Once again, I found myself asking, "Why, God?"

I was going to have to deal with the abuse of my son. I had taken on the responsibility to be a mother. I brought children into the world, and I needed to protect them. I had criticized my parents for not doing right by me. Now, I was doing the same thing and worse to my own children. I had witnessed the destruction on my son's innocence. Three generations of abuse needed to stop right now.

Coming to terms with this cycle of abuse is difficult. If you can do it successfully, you can break the emotional handcuffs that keep you locked into relationships that are not only bad for you but can also be life-threatening. It is not enough to realize you are damaged, but you have to do something about it. It starts with learning to love your self.

All of the people I had brought into my life were severely flawed. I had the wrong idea about what love really meant. I made bad choices about a whole host of things. I had been shaped and influenced to such a degree by the abuse that sometimes I could not discern right from wrong. This does not excuse me from being mature and making decisions based on common sense, but it explains a lot.

I needed to build up the shaky foundation upon which my personality was built. I had to finally get real about my false ideologies and myths about romantic love. Sure it was possible to love someone, but you had to know what that meant. Clearly, I didn't have any idea about how to go about being in love. Just imagine what I could have been without the constant setbacks. Life is not just about what you deserve. Everyone deserves to be treated with dignity and respect. But you must be able to know that you are due that respect and you yourself must be willing to own the responsibility for demanding it in your relationships with everyone. I was living proof of the adage that you get what you expect. Well, I expected the worst, and I got it.

Taxi Ride

I found myself trying to start over again after my breakup with Eric. I felt my children were safe, I had a decent job, and I had managed to save some money. The financial pressures decreased, and I did not feel like I needed a man to help me. At my job, I was able to get overtime and my mother was helping out by watching the kids. In spite of this rosier picture, I was still very unhappy with myself. I was only 22 and had already had lived several lifetimes. Over the past eight years I had managed to wear out my body and mind. I was physically and mentally scarred and needing to make a change.

I made a change that made sense to me. I decided to have surgery to improve my body. I always felt I was not attractive. My idea to transform my body was prompted by my persistent desire to be a dancer. I believed that I still had a chance, but I needed to be enhanced to get that chance at proving I could be on stage and make money. My hips were still narrow and my breasts small. The women in the videos didn't look that way. I decided to get breast implants and a tummy tuck.

I thought about how I might become a professional dancer but there were not those kinds of opportunities in Durham. Now that I looked different, my dreams of somehow making it in the videos or on stage did not seem to make so much sense. I thought my enhanced appearance would probably only get me into the door as a topless dancer if I stayed in the area. It would be a way for me to take care of my children without having to depend on a man. However, I had no idea about how to break into that business. That idea was put on hold for another year or so. When starting down that career path I would already look the part.

My job was a meaningful part of my life. I made friends there and some of those relationships have lasted to this day. The first person I met was Jerry. We went out to a local night club together as friends and the friendship has stuck for six years. Jerry would later figure prominently in the events related to the Duke Lacrosse case.

Shortly after meeting Jerry, I met Matthew. I remember the exact date. It was on March 14, 2001, and he has been my one steady and stable boyfriend. He is still a part of my life, and I don't know what I would have done without him. A co-worker introduced Matthew to me. One night this co-worker approached me and said, "I think my man wants to get to know you."

Jokingly, I responded, "Does your man have a name?"

"Yes, his name is Matthew."

I wanted to know who this secret admirer was, "Why doesn't he just tell me if he likes me so much?"

My co-worker did not answer my question. He asked another instead. "Do you live in Durham?"

"Yes, I live on Charles Street."

"That's right around the corner from him," he added.

I was feeling bold. "Why doesn't he take me home then?"

"I'll go ask him," he responded.

A little time later a little short guy made his way down the steps towards me. I was not expecting him to be my admirer. "Someone told me that you needed a ride home." It was Matthew. "Meet me at that door," he pointed, "after work, and I'll take you home."

At the end of the shift, I met Matthew at the door as planned. We got into his car without saying a word. I felt nervous. I had sworn off men since Eric. We rode in silence most of the way. I did not know what to say. Once we got to my parents' house, he parked the car. Matthew turned to me and, out of nowhere, said, "I heard that you have fake breasts. Is it true?"

I wasn't sure what to say. I did have implants and I did draw a lot of attention from men. Matthew then asked me if he could feel them because he had never touched any enhanced breast before. I wasn't sure why but I said that he could touch them. He reached out and gently squeezed my breast. Then he squeezed again. His mouth was agape in fascination.

My first reaction was to slap Matthew, but I had given him permission. I just smiled, said goodbye, and went into the house. I couldn't help but laugh at what just happened. My improvements had gotten me noticed.

The next day at work I went upstairs to talk to Matthew. I was not clear what I wanted to say, but I had been out of the dating game for some time and wanted to try one more time. I know that the way we met was not typical, but I had never had an ordinary beginning to any of my relationships. Just like that, by the time we finished talking, we had made plans to go to the beach for the weekend. He promised he would be a gentleman and even cook me breakfast. This was pretty fast but I had a good feeling about what was happening.

Once we got to the beach I had not expected I would be having sex with Matthew, but I did. It was different than any other time I had sex. It was even better than with Ryan, and I was sure that I had been really in love with him. It felt so good for a change. I did not think about all of the rough treatment I had suffered at the hands of Fred. For the first time in a long time, I had an orgasm. We had sex a lot that weekend, but I was concerned about the pace at which we were moving. I think we stayed in bed from Friday to Sunday.

Since that weekend we have been more than friends. Through ups and downs, breakups and make up, thick and thin, we have managed to make it work somehow. From that point forward Matthew has been included in every major event of my life.

The events of March 2006 and its aftermath have caused a tremendous strain in the relationship, though. I can say I have not suffered physical abuse; however, the strain of the constant media attention and the attacks on my character had an impact. Matthew trusted me and wanted to support me. He knew I had problems in the past with relationships, my mental health, and self-esteem. He worked hard at keeping the relationship together despite what other people thought of me.

That weekend at the beach was the beginning of our relationship. If I was meant to fall in love and have a man in my life, it has to be with Matthew. This time my relationship has not been the source of my sorrow.

Even with Matthew in my life I have still had moments of unhappiness. Everything was not going to be fixed in that one weekend. I had a major depressive episode in June 2002. With Father's Day approaching, I felt badly that my children were not seeing their own father. I knew they needed to have a relationship with their father, but he had chosen to not to be a part of their lives. I knew how important having good parental relationships were, and I felt especially concerned for my son. I was still feeling guilt about what happened to RJ. In a deeply depressed state, I went on a terrible drinking binge.

I got over that depression, but I still could not feel happy. Matthew was there for me and despite having a good job, starting college, and having a good relationship I felt my children were not getting what they needed. I thought that if I had more money our lives would be easier. I decided that I could put my cosmetic surgery to work. I was finally going to be a dancer.

I know it does not seem to make any sense. My plan was illogical and I knew Matthew wouldn't think it was such a great idea. I had to find a way to introduce him to my plan and try to convince him it would be a good move. I asked Matthew to go to a strip club on Angier Avenue in Durham to see what it was like. He reluctantly agreed.

I talked to the manager and expressed my interest in going on stage. I needed to get my courage up so I did what I would come to do a lot: I drank. As a matter of fact, I had a few too many drinks and I got into an argument with Matthew. He did not want to be in the club in the first place, and he had every right to be mad. I was drunk and he was so angry about what was happening that he left me at the club without a ride home. Alone and drunk, the manager approached me and said I could go up on stage to dance and show him what I had. I did dance to a few songs. I thought I hadn't done so badly, but I was not so sure.

This was a long way from being a ballerina, but I thought it was the first step in moving ahead.

After a while, when I realized that Matthew was gone, I started to cry. I was drunk and alone. One of the ladies at the club came over to console me and calm me down. She let me know there was a man there offering to give me a ride home. I went to the dressing room to get dressed and the man met me at the door. "I need to go to check on my children," I told him. "I'm really worried about them."

The man handed me a set of keys. He was as drunk as I was. "The car over there," he pointed me in the direction of his car. Before I knew it, I was behind the wheel of a car and pulling out of the driveway of the club.

A voice came out of nowhere. "Car 15, are you there?"

"What was that?" I thought. I didn't realize I was driving a taxi cab. I should not have been driving anything.

I headed towards Raleigh with no headlights shining. I was going the opposite direction when I should have headed home which was not that far from the club. By now the taxi cab has been reported stolen, and soon the sirens came. There were police cars in hot pursuit.

I felt a jolt of sobriety. I thought, "Why me?" I just wanted to get home to my kids. I could not think about anything else right now. I needed to keep driving. Police cruisers were all around me and forced me into a parking lot. I sat there quietly for a moment, but then the alcohol started talking to me, "Back up now!" I did but there happened to be a police car behind me. I crashed into the police cruiser. The criminal charges were starting to mount, and I had no clue.

Before the night was over, I was charged with multiple crimes. The two felonies and five misdemeanors that are now part of my record are public and there is nothing to hide. But the story is vastly different than reflected by the record that has been used to discredit me to the present:

- Felonious Assault with a Deadly Weapon on Police Officer, O2-CRS-49961
- Felonious Larceny and Felonious Possession of Stolen Vehicle charges, 02-CRS-49955
- Felonious Speeding to Elude Arrest,
- Driving while Impaired (.19 Blood Alcohol Content) and Driving while License Revoked, 02-CRS-49956
- Driving Left of Center, 02-CR-49958
- Failure to Heed Blue Light and Siren and Reckless Driving in Wanton Disregard to Rights or Safety of Others, 02-CR-49959
- Driving the Wrong Way on Dual Lane Highway and Open Container After Consuming Alcohol, 02-CR-49960
- Two counts of Injury to Personal Property, 02-CR-49962-63
- Resisting a Public Officer, 02-CR-49964

Everyone who has had an opinion of me declares I stole a car and led police on a high-speed chase. I suppose that is what it is. There is no excuse for what happened. The damages were $10,000 and $5,000 in attorney's fees.

I went to court and took my punishment. I put people's lives in danger. I was never an ex-convict, as various people have portrayed. I was not sent to the North Carolina Women's prison or anything like that. I was put on probation and did community service. I was 22-years-old and completely confused about what I should be doing with my life. I regret that episode everyday of my life.

My incident with the police caused me to step back and make another plan. I was having a terrible time finding a job. My options were limited. I decided to concentrate on getting an education. I had wanted that in the first place. I knew I was capable and my family had expected me to do that prior to joining Navy.

I enrolled in Durham Technical College to pursue an associate degree. I put everything I had into my school work at Durham Tech and did well. Matthew and I were also doing well. For the first time in a long time, there was no abuse and no major upheaval. He forgave my indiscretions at the strip club and knew I would not have stolen a taxi club for the hell of it. If it not for Matthew it would have been difficult for me to make it through the turmoil.

In March 2004 I went back to work. I eventually found someone who would look past my criminal record and give me a chance to work as a medical technician at an adult care facility. I thought I wanted to be a nurse and this new job was a perfect fit. My education at Durham Tech continued, and I could finally think about reaching a real goal. My plan was to finish my associate degree and enroll at North Carolina Central University to get my bachelor's degree.

Things went well at my job at the adult care facility for about a year but the management changed. I was assigned to a new manager and a new role. All of the changes made going to work stressful, but I tried to stay positive. I would be finished at Durham Tech soon and going off to NCCU. But I could never seem to agree with anything my manager said. I thought she was going out of her way to make things difficult for me. I was told that I was not professional because I smiled all of the time. I guess that's just a nervous tic I had developed over time. I always smile a lot. Because I smiled all the time, she said I was unreliable. That did not make sense to me, but I was not going to argue. I needed the job, so I was going to try and avoid a confrontation at all cost. Everything came to a head when during the last shift I would work there, my manager asked me to do something. As usual I didn't say anything contrary. I smiled and turned away to go do what was asked.

"Did you hear me?" my manager asked.

"Yes," I turned around and smiled again.

She could no longer contain herself and went into a rage. I kept my composure and walked away without saying another word. At the end of my shift, I was called into the manager's office and informed that I was being let go. I held my emotions until I got home. I really did like my job, and it had meant so much that someone had given me a chance after my legal problems.

I did discover that after I was let go many patients commented on how much they had liked me. That made me feel good. I knew that I was giving my best effort while I was there and making the patients comfortable was important to me. I knew they appreciated it, and they told me often. Being nice to people allowed me to receive kindness back from them. A lot of times knowing that I was helping people and making them smile was the only thing that kept me going to work. School was challenging and I wanted to finish so not having to work actually eased some of my stress. I just did not like having to leave my job under these circumstances.

The one good thing was that I had Matthew with me during this latest crisis. We were living together by April 2005, and needed to move into a larger house in a safer neighborhood for the sake of the children. But the higher rent and escalating bills were too much for Matthew to carry on his own. I regretfully suggested that I give exotic dancing another try. This time Matthew agreed. We needed to do something drastic and my criminal record was too hard to explain. I had to finish school to get a better chance. Of course, this would go down as one more bad decision I would make, but at the time it seemed a reasonable idea. I did not act on it right away. I needed to find the right way to get involved this time.

Three months after losing my job, I once again fell into a deep depression. I hate to admit it, but whenever I'm feeling like a failure all the emotions associated with the past abuses I've suffered boil to the surface. I feel inferior and turn to drinking. We had bills to pay and I was pressing to finish school. It was June 2005, and I needed to figure out how to get out of the funk I was in. Even with how I was feeling I was able to finish at Durham Tech and had started making plans for enrolling the upcoming fall at NCCU. My depression was so serious that I felt I needed some intervention. I checked myself into Holly Hills Hospital.

Holly Hills specializes in treating mental health disorders, and I felt I really needed to be there. During my two-week inpatient stay, the staff diagnosed me with bipolar disorder. They prescribed medication that seemed to work well, and I began to feel better almost immediately.

After being released from Holly Hills, my family physician, Dr. Rogers, disagreed with the assessment they made at the hospital. His diagnosis was major depression with periodic reoccurrences. My medication was changed. I was told to stop taking the mood-altering drugs and to take only the ones that would treat the depression. I was following the advice of the doctors despite my uncertainty about which drugs were appropriate. I still felt okay and there was no immediate change in my mental health state. My main concern was the question of how was I going to raise my two children, go to college, and maintain a household with Matthew if I did not have a job.

Of course, I wanted to dance long before my life got crazy and out of control. I sincerely believed that if I had a chance I could make it as a dancer. My constant search for love coupled with the string of broken relationships and abuse by men had taken a toll. I really had no clue what professional dancing was. I had never taken the time to find out. I was still stuck in my youthful illusion of being a ballerina or video girl. I had wasted my time chasing other unrealistic dreams. Unknowingly, I had the ability within myself all of the time to be whatever I wanted to be, but I had squandered every opportunity.

I never thought that the thing that had always seemed to make me happy—dancing—could be so exploitative and detestable. I had gone into this thinking that the only difference between professional dancing in videos and on stage at the strip club was that the exotic dancers made more money. I really believed that people stood at the stage and threw handfuls of money at you. My previous one-day dance career had not done anything to change my impression of what the exotic dancing was about. What would change my mind was meeting one of the girls in the club named Nikki (not Kim Pittman aka Kim Roberts).

Nikki was a slightly built girl. Out of her dancing gear and her wig, she was tomboyish. She reminded me a lot of myself. She was my one friend at The Platinum Pleasure Club.

We talked about her very difficult upbringing and her life story tugged at my heartstrings. She told me about years of sexual abuse and how her dancing career started at age 13. Her mother died when she was younger. Her father was nowhere to be found. As a result she was passed around between any family member who would take her in. Some of her own relatives took advantage of her sexually. The constant abuse left her confused and feeling abandoned. She was eventually introduced to dancing as a way to feed and take care of herself.

In addition to dancing, Nikki sold her body to anyone who would pay. The gig at the Platinum Pleasures Club was extra money for her pimp. Her pimp was a tall man with dreadlocks who would bring Nikki to the club. He kept three girls at his house, including Nikki. In the time she was not at the club, Nikki worked on the streets in Raleigh with the other girls. Usually selling herself all day and then coming to the club at night. Luckily for Nikki, she was not on hard drugs. Her work for her pimp netted her a place to stay, some food, and a bag of marijuana on an occasion. Nikki told me she turned over everything she made tricking to her pimp. That was the same for the other girls he owned.

Hearing Nikki's story was just plain horrible. She was a beautiful woman when she dressed up. If she put on makeup and attached her wig, she was glamorous. She could have been a legitimate entertainer or a great singer. Even so, she was not able to see a way out of the lifestyle. Her pimp controlled every aspect of her life and convinced her she could not go anywhere. By the time I met Nikki in early 2006, she had been in the game for almost 10 years.

I had suffered a lot of sexual abuse, but I could not even begin to imagine what Nikki had gone through. The worst story she ever told me was about the day she spent turning tricks all day in Raleigh. She had been with a series of men and had managed to make about 500 dollars. She would have to turn the entire amount over to her pimp at the end of the day, then head over to the club for several hours more of lap dances. Wanting to turn one more trick, Nikki got into the car of a man who took her into an alley behind a building. Thinking this was going to be a quick session of oral sex, she was shocked when the john pulled a gun and demanded all of her money. He had been watching her all day and realized that she would be an easy target. Surely, she could not tell the police and say she had been robbed of her money she had earned turning tricks. Her bigger problem was what would she tell her pimp.

Nikki told me how all she could do was cry. I had never turned tricks before, but I knew what it was like to be used. All of the times Fred had sex with me it was as if I was being robbed. I was giving everything I had of me every time he raped me but not once did I get anything in return. I felt so sorry for Nikki and wanted so much to help her, but I could not help myself. It was difficult for me to do what I was doing without feeling some guilt. What must it have been like for Nikki?

I still think about Nikki and hope she finds a way out. I tell Nikki's story because I do not want anyone to get the impression that I have anything against women in the business. Every single person I met is a human being struggling to take care of basic needs. For the ones like Nikki who were doing prostitution, their youth had been turned completely upside down due to sexual exploitation.

Finally, there was nothing elegant about what I saw behind stage as an exotic dancer. On stage I suppose dancers did have to show a good deal of athleticism, gracefulness, acting, and personality all at once, but it was emotionally challenging. Many had children. Some were trying to put themselves through school like me. Others had felony convictions, mental health problems, and drug and alcohol issues. They did not have many other alternatives for employment.

Now that I am away from the club scene, I also look at videos in a different way. Watching all of those images in the music videos can distort a girl's view of dancing. All of the videos show beautiful women living in mansions with rich rap stars. Some of the girls start to believe they could be one of them. Lounging by the pool, sitting on the hood of an expensive car to "pop, lock, and drop it like it's hot" is a fantasy. Being surrounded by men who adore them and would throw thousands of dollars in cash at them is not real.

What young girls see when their parents are not watching has to have a profound impact on how they decide what is acceptable. The videos that are being shown today are much worse than those just a decade ago. Many of the current songs and the accompanying videos glamorize exotic dancing.

Being on stage in some club, whether it is upscale or seedy, is not okay. On account of my firsthand experience, there are some lessons I learned and want to impart to anyone reading this who believes exotic dancing might be for them. I will say it again: This kind of work is not about dancing gracefully and effortlessly. It is nothing like being a ballerina. The men and women there do not think much of you. You will not become rich or even be able to be self-supporting. There are people there who want you to become dependent on drugs and alcohol, so they can take what you do earn. You will not find meaningful relationships. The people who patronize the clubs are there to use you for their sexual gratification. Those are the realities and any of the other women who have survived the life can tell you the same thing.

As fate would have it, I ran into one of my high school friends, Milton. I had known him since we were 14 and when we met we clicked, but not in a sexual way. We were just cool with each other. I had Matthew at home and he was good to me. There was no reason to step out on him. Besides, Milton was married but was estranged from his wife. I became a sounding board for him, and we talked often about what was bothering each one of us. We also had catching up to do. By now I was 27, he was 29. Milton and I started to hang out more, he introduced me to some of his friends, and he took me to some of his hangouts around Durham. During one of our get-togethers I was complaining about how tight things were. Money was always a source of concern because Matthew was carrying the entire load. I still had not followed up on my plan to start dancing to supplement the family's income but Milton said he knew exactly how I could get started.

"I know about this night club and the girls there don't stress about paying their bills," Milton told me. He went on, "You like to dance, don't you? And you said you wanted to try it. I think they have an amateur night on Friday, and I think you should come." He told me he went there all of the time and sometime would blow his entire paycheck. Due to the amount of money he spent there, Milton was a VIP customer and entitled to special benefits. That meant Milton also knew the owner of the club; he could pull some strings if I needed it.

Milton and I took the 20-minute drive northwest of Durham off Interstate 85. He introduced me to the manager and told him I wanted to dance. The owner of the club was a man named Victor. Milton assured him I was cut out for the job and with that I was told to come back the next day to dance. I was hired on the spot.

The night Milton and I went to the club business was very slow. There was only one girl on stage and only a few customers. One customer was leaving when Milton and I were talking with Victor. He let it be known that he was disappointed with the entertainment. As for the girls I met that night, most seemed happy with what they were doing and bragged about how much money they were making. I had no way of knowing things were different until I became a regular dancer and was able to go backstage.

Having gotten over the first hiring hurdle, my plan was to work long enough to get caught up on all the bills and have some left over to do some things for the kids. The money was great from the start. The only problem was I could not drive because of the taxi cab incident. Matthew could not bring me every night because someone had to watch the kids. Milton, Matthew, and I conjured up a plan that they would take turns bringing me with two other friends, Jerry and David.

The more I could go to the club, the more I could make. It was great at first. My kids could have nice things, the rent was getting paid, and I had enough to take care of the guys getting me to work, But the more I made, the more I needed.

The more time I spent at the club, the more I could see it was not so great after all. At first I was concentrating so much on myself and the money that I paid little attention to the women around me. My intuition was getting to me, that feeling of approaching trouble. It was February 2006 and the infamous "bachelor party" was about a month away.

In the meantime at the club, I began really noticing the women working there. There were women around me who were passing out from drugs or drink. Women there lived with abusive boyfriends or pimps like Nikki. They were catty and territorial because dancers had to compete for the customers' attention or they didn't make any money. The rules were clear—even your best friend was your enemy inside the club.

The taxi cab incident was an early warning sign, but I had convinced myself that it was in the past. Everyone working in the club or going there to patronize it was out for him or herself.

Of course I told myself that I was different. I was a professional dancer, and I had a support system that would help me get through whatever I needed. The other girls didn't have people like Matthew and Milton to make sure things were taken care of. Nevertheless, if you hang around that kind of environment long enough it will start rubbing off on you. You cannot help but be influenced by all of the negative stuff that goes on. Plus, I was carrying my own dark secrets.

I told myself I was not planning on being in the game long. There was an end to this for me because I still planned on finishing college and getting a degree. I could walk away from this when the pressure of school was off. My heart ached for some of the girls, and I knew they were damaged. I worried about some of the customers, too, because some, like Milton, were constantly pouring their money into the girls, and to what end? This environment was harsh in tone and atmosphere.

One of the most heartbreaking things for me was to see one dancer who still came to the club although she was pregnant. I figured she had to be six months along, but you could not tell. Not only was she expecting a baby, but she was also behind on her rent and she had a fiendish cocaine habit. Imagine what it takes to put yourself on a stage, exhibiting yourself in front of people who don't care whether you are your baby survives.

As much as I detested what was going on at times, I could not help but like what the money offered. The lifestyle, the fast money, men falling all over themselves to meet and be with you was a rush. The game of getting men to part with their hard-earned paychecks could be a thrill sometimes. It has a twisted way of pulling you in for more. It is about winning and losing as the women compete for every customer and every dollar in their pocket.

The dancer is addicted to the money as if it was a drug. Moreover, some of the customers can become addicted to you and obsessed with the dancer. You are literally putting you life at risk. Some of the customers really believe you like them and will not back off. The more you give, the more they want.

You do whatever it takes to get deeper in their pockets, but you have to know where to draw the line. I did not want to be just a piece of meat, and I'm sure that cost me money. I did not want to have a price tag on me or appear that I could be bought for the right price. Matthew was still at home.

March 13, 2006—Part Two

My career at the Platinum Pleasure Club was bringing in a good deal of money. In addition to that, I took an extra gig with Bunnyhole Entertainment run by Tammy and Melissa. Going into my second month as a professional exotic dancer, everyday I saw more and more things I did not like. Now I was at this party at 610 Buchanan Boulevard with a room full of obnoxious young guys.

The night had not started out well and our retreat to the car after the broomstick incident should have been the end of the night. But we were back in the house and things worsened. It was and still is very difficult to remember every detail. Emotionally upset, I felt dizzy and out of sorts when we returned to the house.

My account of what happened next is the same as I have described all along. It has been said that I gave varying accounts but that just isn't true. People have written reports who did not interview me directly. Why are they more credible than I am? Because defending sexual assault cases is calling into question the accuser's account.

It is established that perfect recall of any traumatic event is never exact. It comes down to the two sides fighting as hard as they can to win their freedom. Yes, the accuser in the case is looking for freedom, too. Carrying the weight of a sexual assault on a person is a devastating burden.

What I am about to describe is what I remember to the best of my ability. I know people want me to name names and point fingers but that would just be opening up a whole can of worms. The criminal case is closed! But that does not mean I do not believe I was violated. It just means that there is no way for me do any more about it.

Kim/Nikki and I got separated. I was forced into the bathroom with three of the partygoers, grabbed by the throat, and quickly subdued. There were two people in front of me and one in the back. I tried to pull away but one of them grabbed my arm and pulled me back. The one holding my arm said, "Sweetheart, you can't leave." He then stood behind me while another man stood in the front. I could hear yelling in the other room. I screamed, too, hoping someone would hear me but the noise coming from the other room was very loud.

The more I tried to break away the tighter they held on to me. I was in a great deal of pain. Then I felt as though I was being penetrated, first in my vagina and then in my anus. I tried to focus on other things while being attacked. "Next!" my first attacker said.

The second attacker was now standing in front of me as the first held me from behind. "What are you going to do?" he said. "Are you going to be still or am I going to have to kill you?" He penetrated my vagina. I pulled at his shirt trying to make him stop. Quickly he was done. From all of the struggling my tightly glued fingernails began to pop loose, causing my fingertips to have a burning sensation.

The three attackers exchanged words. I don't remember all that was said because there was still a lot of noise coming from the other room. However, I could make out what the third attacker said. "I don't want to. I love my fiancé and we are going to get married."

The other two attackers coaxed him into taking his turn. When he finally did, each thrust hurt and it felt like my insiders were being ripped out. I also believe I may have been penetrated with a foreign object. I genuinely believed I was going to die in there, but I did not want to.

The second attacker decided to penetrate me again. This time anally and painfully. He removed himself just before he had an orgasm and ejaculated on the floor.

Minutes following that attack, I heard Kim/Nikki's voice. The guys wiped me off quickly and attempted to straighten my clothes. Nikki entered the bathroom and helped them finish fixing my clothes. I wanted to run out of there, and I tried. The guys wanted me out of there, too. Nikki and I eventually made it to the back door and out of the house. The next thing I remember is having difficulty standing and several people dragging me towards Nikki's car. I was afraid and did not know what to do. They put me in the front passenger seat.

I sat in the car with my eyes closed and pretended to be asleep. Nikki got out of the car and when no one was looking I started to cry. I could tell she was yelling at the guys but I could not make out what she was saying.

Nikki got back in the car and as we were driving off she asked me if I was okay. I told her that I had been attacked. I did not know where my things were. My cell phone, my bag, and the money were gone.

I am not sure how long we drove around. I did not know Nikki other than in the brief time we had been together that night. She had no idea where I lived, and I could not tell her where to take me because I was not exactly sure where I was. I was still feeling sick and disoriented. Nikki said she did not know what to do, and finally she pulled into a Kroger parking lot.

She went inside and talked with a security guard. She wanted me out of the car, but I would not leave. I was scared and did not know what to do. The records and 911 tapes are clear that the police were called, and soon they arrived at the store parking lot.

I remember being taken to Duke Medical Center, where I was given a mild sedative and I drifted off to sleep. Around 3:00 am when I awoke there was a nurse in the room asking questions and writing down my answers quickly on a note pad.

Later, a lady named Amy from the Durham Rape Crisis Center visited me. She was a true angel and one of the nicest people I've ever met. I had a pelvic exam that was excruciating. I was in so much pain that it took them a long time to complete the examination.

I didn't phone Matthew until the next morning about 9:00 am. I was still feeling stunned at what had happened when I called to tell him of my whereabouts. I could not come right out and tell him the details. "What's wrong?" he asked. I didn't want to answer. How could I tell him that I had been violated? I was afraid it would ruin our relationship. Even though I had been an exotic dancer, I had never been violated like this since I had been with Matthew. We had a deal that I could dance if things stayed in control but this had gotten completely out of hand.

It would take nearly 15 hours for me to be released from the hospital. My time being treated and evaluated was six times longer than the entire time I was supposed to spend dancing in that house. I considered this episode a sign to me that none of the monies I could ever make dancing was worth the risk. Not only did I spend all that time being examined, I have had two years of constant scrutiny. There is no telling how many more years I'll have to relive the trauma.

After all of this time, I still have difficulty believing that I was the person being examined. Not because I do not believe I was there but because so many people speak with so much certainty about my physical and mental state as if they were there.

Obviously, I am not an expert on the mental health of sexual assault victims. I only know how I felt before, during, and after I was raped prior to the North Buchanan incident. I do vividly remember my attackers from my teenage years. I had no choice because I was in love with one of the men who brutalized me repeatedly. I also remember the other men well enough to discuss their physical stature and their behavioral characteristics. The events at the 610 North Buchanan are a different matter all together. I had all of 10 minutes to know everything about everyone who may or may not have come in and out of that house, particularly the bathroom. Those were faces of people I had never seen and would never likely see again. I was in surroundings I had never been in before.

Realistically, what should a victim be able to remember? What is the history in other cases like mine? I just know that my emotions were all over the place. It was especially troubling because I made the choice about dancing in the first place. I was only supposed to be doing this so that I could better myself. I wanted to forget what happened while at the same time I needed to remember so that I could assist the investigators. The first few days of interrogation were a very trying time for me.

From the limited research I have done, I recognize there is a large number of sexual assault victims who cannot remember important details about their rapists.

Lacking videotaped footage of my behavior and physical state, the only thing to go on are the reports from the people who examined me that night. I am convinced that the hospital staff that night did their jobs. I have not spoken to any of them since that night, but I assure you they were not manufacturing the injuries they reported finding on me.

At 5:00 pm the next day, I was discharged. Matthew was there to support me as I found it difficult to walk. My friends helped me to get back and forth to the doctor and other places I needed to go. I did continue to bleed profusely for a few weeks afterwards. It took nearly a week before I was able to walk with my normal gait.

The damage to my body was much more extensive than has ever been reported in the media. I required several X-rays and MRI exams that showed bruising to my neck and knee that were not present before the attack. I had to have pain medication for my neck and wear a knee support. The pain lasted for weeks afterwards.

The next few days following the attacks I felt ashamed of what had happened to me. I stayed inside and was constantly playing back what I could remember. Regardless of whether I was doing routine things around the house or just sitting there, I kept trying to think about how I could have done things differently to prevent this incident from happening. I was deeply troubled by the fact that they had used racial epithets before, during, and after the attack. Their hate crime made me question my relationship with the father of my two children. I began to wonder if Ryan had ever felt the same way as my attackers. Was I a "black bitch" to Ryan when we had sex? I remembered the times I had been intimate with men who had yelled at me, pulled my hair, or called me hateful names even when I was engaged in consensual sex. Did they think I was just a slut, despite my being in love with those men? I felt dirty.

A few days after the party, I was at the Durham Police Department speaking with the investigator. This was the first time I was asked to identify people in a photo lineup. I was shown about 25 pictures. I could not say for sure I recognized any of the people. Some of them looked familiar but these were not people I would know offhand. I was also still angry and upset. The investigators were polite and patient but this was hard. My first attempt to make an identification did not yield anything.

My experience in trying to make an identification should not be looked at as anything other than one individual case.

I would return at least two more times to the Durham Police Department to make an identification in March and then again in early April 2006. Both times I had difficulty for the same reason I've always had. I saw a room full of strangers for maybe 30 minutes that night. The environment was hostile and when doing this kind of work, you are not looking forward to making friends or being around any longer than you need to be.

As for the way the lineups were conducted, I am told they were in violation of standard practice for conducting such procedures. I had no way of knowing that, and I was asked to make identifications based on what was presented to me. I was told that more than likely the people in the pictures were people at the party.

The police didn't coax or coach me. As far as I could tell they were trying as hard as they could to investigate this case. I wanted to get this behind me and had no intention of making this a spectacle. My encounters with the police during the entire time never led me to believe they were trying to create a media circus either. Not once did I have the slightest hint that anything in the investigation was extraordinary. The notion that the Durham Police Department somehow decided that my case was about framing people for no reason seems so crazy. I believed that everyone who talked with me was trying to do his or her job. I certainly did not feel like I was receiving any special treatment.

As I went through each of the photo lineups, I was honest and tried as hard as I could to positively identify who I believed hurt me. Every time I hear that the police conducted the identification process incorrectly, it makes me wonder what happens in other cases? I went to those police interviews on my own and there were no handlers or people influencing me. I was still a student and a mother who needed to take care of her two kids.

In less than a month, the entire episode had blown up into national news. You can best believe I was not in favor of making any of this public. There never should have been cameras following anyone involved in the case, including the individuals who ultimately ended up being charged. It did not help that the attorneys for the lacrosse players called press conferences and appeared on cable talk shows more than anyone else. In their zeal to serve their clients, it seems as though they were calling as much attention to the case as possible. I never once asked anyone to speak publicly on my behalf. I really expected this to work like most cases working through the system. The case would either die for lack of evidence, or I would be sitting on the witness stand giving my testimony.

Once arrests were made on April 18, 2006, the media frenzy accelerated aggressively. Both national and local news outlets were knocking on my door. They had no boundaries and saw nothing wrong with coming at 11:00 pm while I was trying to rest or getting my kids to bed. The reporters and producers would camp out all night and into the next day for what seemed like an eternity. I couldn't live this way. It wasn't right for them to be able to harass a person like this. While the Duke boys and their attorneys sought and bought as much media attention as they could, I wanted no part of it.

I needed to get away and on April 27, 2006, I left my house. I was driven to a safe house by an investigator who told me I needed to collect my thoughts and get away from all of the commotion at my house. I joined two other residents in the house and prayed that this would blow over quickly. I left early that Thursday morning and entrusted my two rat terriers with a family member.

The residents and staff at the facility where I stayed were nice to me. They offered us food and clothing, and we tried to settle in. I got my kids enrolled in a new school for a short time, but as quickly as we moved in we had to move out again. I felt awful and worn down. I thought I was going through another bout of depression, plus I was just plain homesick. I felt too poorly to help out with chores around the house, which was a condition of staying. It was only later that I realized that the fatigue was the result of my being pregnant with a third child.

I do feel I must address several allegations that have become accepted as fact and truth relating to the weeks following the events on March 13. More than a few people from the Platinum Pleasures Club were produced to say that I danced at the club later in March 2006. Those allegations are not true. I never danced again at the club. I did attend a CD-release party for a local act during that time frame, but I was only there briefly. The alleged videotape of me dancing at the club was from several months *before* the incident at 610 North Buchanan. There is evidence that the tape was analyzed and verified something other than what some people wanted to believe.

One other compelling point I would like to air is that the bouncer at the club who said I talked about making money from the Duke boys is telling an outright lie. At the time I was supposed to have said that, four days after the party, I still had no idea who the people were at the party. Moreover, the bouncer was facing drug charges and was being represented by one of the attorneys on the lacrosse players' defense team.

I needed to resume a normal life as best as I could. My children had no real idea what was going on and to some extent I didn't either. I just knew that day after day the story was taking turns and twists as the defense attorneys were constantly attacking Mike Nifong. I was unaware of all of the talk on the Web, the blogs, the speculation about me and my past until much later. Simply, the kids needed to do their homework and I needed to cook dinner. I was pregnant and had to figure out how we were going to manage and how I could finish school. I wasn't obsessed with everything that was going on about the case and it amazed me when I saw the shear number of words devoted to comments on this case.

People can criticize how the district attorney handled the case, but I am not sure he knew what to do either. The truth is I had very little contact with him over the course of the media spectacle. I did not sit down with him for an extensive interview until December 2006. That was about nine months after the party. Of course, I did speak with the investigators a number of times, but it was not as if I was involved day-to-day in the investigation. To this day, I cannot tell you very much about how the Durham Police went about gathering evidence at the scene or who they interviewed about the case. I was waiting for the outcome just like everyone else.

I do need to say something about the DNA evidence in the case. I have seen reports implying that I had multiple sex partners in the days or maybe hours before the incident. This was not proven in the DNA samples that were taken at the hospital. There have been wild reports that semen was found in various orifices of my body. The forensics test done by the State Bureau of Investigations and the DNA lab did not show any semen.

It would be irresponsible for me to try and explain DNA reports that I have not seen and could have no real way of interpreting. Nevertheless, what I can say is that others have exaggerated their unscientific assessments of the DNA reports. The truth is I live with my boyfriend Matthew, and it stands to reason that his DNA would be on me and my clothing. I also performed exotic dancing and there is little question that I came in close contact with men. It is clear to me that the people who have defamed me by suggesting that I was covered in semen all over my body knew what they were doing. It was and still is a part of the attempt to call me a prostitute.

If the DNA confirms that none of the people charged left DNA on me, then the test performed their function. I cannot and will not argue with that. Nevertheless, I believe there are DNA tests in the case file that may tell a different story. Unfortunately, with the case file not being public record, we can only go on what the defense attorneys want to release to the public. Since there is no chance that a criminal case will go to trial in this matter, I am calling for Attorney General Roy Cooper to release all of the records to the public. Perhaps once and for all it would clear up any misconceptions about what DNA really exists.

Calling for the entire case file to be made public is not something I take lightly. I know there are pictures and video that will not flatter me. Unfortunately, I do not believe there will be any clarity in the case unless everything is finally exposed. I am willing to take that risk. Can everyone at that party on March 13, 2006, say the same thing? Little, if any, real information about what was said and done at the party has ever been made public. *Instead the discussions have always been about what did not happen.* So, I have to be skeptical when I hear people from the attorney general's office say that the records are being suppressed in the interest of the public. Yet attorneys in the civil cases against the city of Durham and all kinds of other people have been free to release fragments of the case files to support their cause and continue to influence the public opinion.

Would people feel different about things if they realized that a hate crime was committed against me? If nothing else, there is ample enough evidence to prove that racial slurs were used during my time in that house. I held no animosity against the boys because of their race, then or now, but people at the party used racial slurs to hurt me.

I know these events will follow me the rest of my life if I do not deal with them now. The only thing I stand to gain now is some dignity. Long after everyone has forgotten about the Duke Lacrosse case, I will always wake up knowing that something happened to me and it went unpunished. I also realize that a lot of people believe they have suffered, too. Nevertheless, I have felt stifled and unable to talk on account of all of the vitriol directed at me. It still does not matter that I never did want or ever would want anyone to suffer injustice on my behalf.

I will be forever labeled "the accuser." I cry sometimes and cannot sleep because I think about how others have profited from my pain and suffering.

After years of abuse at the hands of people I knew and brought into my life, I am now being abused by people who do not know me. A good number of people have even been able to profit from the case by writing books, selling movie scripts, and having advertisements on their Web site. The level of scrutiny this case got because of its association with the name of Duke University is beyond comprehension.

I am not sure when and how people outside the police department found out about the party. I do know it did not take long. I used to think that everything that I saw on the six o'clock news was the truth. A reporter from *The N&O* showed up at my door and said she wanted to get my story out. Not knowing any better, I talked to her. It was a terrible mistake. I had never dealt with any media before. How was I to know that things would escalate the way that they did? My boyfriend Matthew did strongly caution it was wrong to talk to anyone. Since then, I have not talked to another journalist except my co-author and CNN.

No one had ever told me that the media is the main source of power. Those who have the most control and influence over public opinion control the media outlets. Having first-hand experience about how it feels to be splashed across every newspaper and on every cable channel, I know this is something you would never wish for.

I cannot say much more about the immediate aftermath, when and how the police collected evidence from the scene. I did not participate in any of that. I know only what the general public knows from the reports on television. It is dismaying to know the police did not go into the house until two days after the party. People would have plenty of time to clean the house of evidence. There was also time to contaminate evidence as well. But how are we to know anything? With the records from the case being sealed, the only people who have any real knowledge about what truly happened in those two days are the people at the party. However, the police did find my bag, cell phone, and fingernails at the house. There was a reason they were there. I told the investigators they would find those things and more.

I also believe the police found one other DNA sample that has rarely been mentioned in any news accounts. That sample was found near the sink in the bathroom. From what I was told, it was semen from one of the individuals who had been at the party. Again, we will never know unless the case file is made public.

After *The N&O* story ran, media from everywhere descended on Durham. In the aftermath when I flipped on the television, I was amazed at what I saw—a slew of people protesting on my behalf. They were marching on campus at Duke and carrying signs. In the days ahead, people would be banging pots and pans on the lawn of the house at 610 North Buchanan. Who were these people and why were they there? I did not know a single person who had organized the protest. I just stood in stunned silence. Besides being stunned, I was also embarrassed. If protesting was going on, it meant people knew that something had happened to me at that house. My story had gotten out and grew larger than anything I could have ever imagined.

In the early morning of the incident, I told the police what I remembered. In every subsequent interview with people such as Detective Himan I told them what I remembered. When the reporter from *The N&O* showed up at the house I told her my story from what I could remember. At the time I thought I was doing the right thing.

Until that point I had not talked to anyone beyond my family about specifics of that night because I thought the police were handling it.

Seeing all the media reports temporarily gave me a bit of hope. If people were concerned, it might help bring the case to closure quicker. My spirit was bolstered because that meant I would have some support to get through this.

It was always strange to see that people such as Jesse Jackson, Al Sharpton, professors at Duke, and many others who either spoke on television or went to the house at 610 North Buchanan to make statements. I really started to worry when none of them actually came to my house to talk to me and offer assistance. If they were so concerned, why had I never met any of them? Everyone had something to say about me, even my so-called supporters, but all of the support was from a distance.

For weeks every time I turned on the television, there was another report. I was still having nightmares where I replayed the events of the attack in my mind. I could almost feel the compression against my neck. I thought about how difficult it was for me to breathe as one of my attackers pulled me into the bathroom.

All of the media attention felt as traumatizing as being raped. To see people speculate about your credibility, talk about your private medical records, and openly accuse you of lying was incredibly difficult. There were journalists who talked as if they were in the bathroom with me, going over every detail. There were those who suggested that I had fantasized about being raped and victimized by powerful men.

So, by the middle of April 2006, I went into another bout of deep depression. It was a day after my daughter's seventh birthday. I felt isolated with irrational fears and an overwhelming feeling of distrust for everyone. I remembered every time I had been taunted, teased, and abused in the past, and I expected everyone was out to get me.

There was a disproportionate sense of balance concerning everything related to this case. With so many people issuing press releases and going on television, you would have believed this was as important as the Iraq War. There was no putting things back to the way they were. I planned to cooperate fully with the police and Mike Nifong.

My biggest gripe—a fair trial? How was that possible? There were people openly arguing the case in public without the one person who could answer most of the questions. That was me!

Another thing that disturbed me about all of the coverage is how the media dealt with my family. There was absolutely no justification for putting any of my family on television to talk about any aspects of the case. It has only been since the later part of 2007 that I have even discussed many of the details with people close to me other than my boyfriend. I was livid when I saw news reporter after news reporter shoving a microphone into the faces of my father or my cousin Jackie.

I never gave permission to my family to talk about what was going on. There was no way for any of the answers my father provided to shed any light on the case.

What my father did say only helped to perpetuate the story that I was somehow so mentally disturbed that I was making all of this up to gain attention. My father spoke from the heart about the difficult times I had with mental health issues, but he isn't a doctor and no one should have been looking to him to evaluate my mental health state. I was angry when I saw those reports, but I do not believe my father was intentionally looking to harm me. He was trying to defend me the best way he knew how, but it was without my approval.

The news outlets that ran stories with my father or cousins should be ashamed. I think he did not know that he could have declined to comment when news crews showed up at his house. He was pressured to say something, and I believe the reporters and producers convinced him that he could help my cause by saying something.

Case Closed

I went back to school and kept myself on track to graduate because I knew those two hours on North Buchanan did not define my entire life. The only way for any event in your life to become a defining moment for you is for you to let it be one. You have to own that moment or let it guide everything you do. I refuse to let this hang around my neck like a stone.

I was cooperating in a continuing investigation and had no personal animosity against anyone. I still don't have anything against anyone. Things happened and I want everyone to stop using this as a reason to support their own cause.

Consequently, I wondered if those same people who were so set on exposing me were searching the newspapers around the country and reviewing every ongoing rape case. Were they trying to discredit every accuser if her background was not perfect? What if every detail had been revealed about everyone who was at the party that night? It is the most troubling part of this entire thing for me that there was so much outside interference.

There was one occasion that really frightened me. While going to pick my kids up from school, I noticed several cars following me. Every turn I made the cars turned right behind me. One of the cars pulled beside me and I was shocked to see a man hanging out the window with a camera. I wondered, was he a private investigator or someone from a tabloid trying to take my picture? Either way it scared me and I hit the gas. They followed me around Durham and I even called to police for help. I was told there was nothing the police could do unless they hurt me. I eventually pulled onto a side street and into a cul-de-sac and started blowing my car horn to attract attention. When the people in their houses started to come out, the would-be paparazzi backed off. Nothing that happened at 610 North Buchanan justified putting anyone's life in danger like that.

People can criticize how Mike Nifong conducted himself in the case. I would have preferred that he never made any statements because everything he was saying about the case was essentially in support of me. It looked as though I had a close relationship with the district attorney. The lawyers arrayed against him were formidable and put the kind of time and resources into the case that had been rarely seen in North Carolina.

Much has been made about Mike Nifong talking about the case in public. It provided a platform for the defense attorneys to gain as much exposure as the district attorney's office. The more time they could spend on television, the more chances they could beat up on everyone in the Durham Police Department, the mayor's office, and the district attorney.

I had no way of gauging whether the case was unraveling internally in the Durham Police Department or with Mike Nifong. Nobody ever came to me directly to express any concerns.

Throughout the summer and fall of 2006 I would occasionally explore what was going on with the case. I was still thinking about how to finish up school. I had to devote my thoughts to making sure my new baby girl would get here safely. I knew many of the television cable shows and radio talk shows would be eventually moving on to other things, but they would always find time to comment on why they believed Mike Nifong was the worst prosecutor ever. I experienced the same treatment as Mr. Nifong, but I tried to ignore untrue comments. I was still holding out hope that there would be a trial or the investigation be allowed to continue.

Of course I did speak with the investigators from time to time but eventually that contact became minimal. The campaign to discredit everyone and everything was in full effect and there was little that could be done to stop things.

During that whole time, I had to tell myself that talking to the media, going on one of the talk shows, or giving an exclusive interview to anyone would be counterproductive. I had very few people around me that I could trust. There was too much risk involved. I wasn't thinking about my reputation because that had already been called into question. I was thinking about the exposure my children would face. I was also concerned about the amount of turmoil that the situation had already created, and I didn't want my community to go through any more.

So, despite the offers to appear on major talk shows and proposals to buy rights to my story, I turned them all down. I had to remind myself that this was not about money. That was a difficult decision to make when Matthew was struggling to put food on the table and with another mouth to feed on the way. Nevertheless, I was standing on principle. I had also started going back to church to seek spiritual guidance. My pastor told me time and again that "the Lord will make a way." I had to pray really hard and hope that my pastor was telling me the truth. Remember, I felt deeply that the Lord had let me down once before, and it was a struggle to give church another chance. I had no choice this time.

I wanted the case to be handed over to someone else beside Nifong. It was not because I did not like Mike Nifong. I believed that things were so out of hand that the only way to come to any conclusion was to have a special prosecutor. I was even willing to accept the fact that rape charges were dropped. There were still charges of kidnapping and sexual assault pending. I felt that if we could at least be given a chance to get to court and I got on the stand, people would be able to see that this was not a witch hunt against "innocent college boys." I know now that the entire identification process was questionable, but I believed then and now that Mike Nifong was not directing anyone to harm anyone else. He was always kind and polite. I never saw or heard anything that made me believe he was doing this for any other reason than this was his job.

The critics had been calling on Mike Nifong to do something. Now that he had by reducing the charges, it still wasn't enough. Before I got a chance to adapt to the new charges, the North Carolina Bar was coming after Mr. Nifong for bringing the charges. What in the world was happening now? Now I really started to think this was a witch hunt, but not the one many on the side of the defense were blogging and talking about. When were we going to put everything on the table?

So, when the case was turned over to Attorney General Roy Cooper, I was pleased. I thought they would continue to pursue the case on the revised charges. After all, I knew enough to realize that people get charged with a higher crime all the time and then the charges get reduced after further investigation. I felt then that the case really had not been investigated on account of all of the other things going around it, such as conflicting and confusing interviews with people like Kim/Nikki Roberts who was trying to get 15 minutes of fame at my expense.

Because 99 per cent of my interactions were with the investigators in the case, I was led to believe they were making progress and had enough information to make whatever case needed. I tried to provide the information they requested. I was now ready to do the same thing with the attorney general.

When the case was switched to the special prosecutor, I believed that their role was to take over for Mike Nifong and prepare the case for trial. I never thought that the case was not going forward.

My first meeting with Mary Winstead and Jim Coman of the attorney general's office went well. Both Mary Winstead and Jim Coman struck me as professional people, but I was a bit nervous. I thought that they were representing me and I did not expect them to be hostile. Mary Winstead introduced herself first and commented that she knew Mike Nifong and expressed that she had confidence in his ability as a district attorney. The impression I got from her was that she was going to do everything she could to help.

Jim Coman seemed to be more matter-of-fact than Mary Winstead. Though not unfriendly, he talked about what we needed to do to move the case forward. Jim Coman told me, "The most important thing to me is to say you don't know rather than to guess when I ask you a question."

I had always tried to say what I remembered and not guess when I had talked to everyone. Going back to the time I initially entered the emergency room at Duke until the first meeting with them, I thought I had said I did not know when I really did not know. However, I was always encouraged to provide some sort of answer even when I was not completely certain about something. I did not know a lot of things for sure just due to the way things happened. I wanted to make sure I could answer everything asked truthfully and to the best of my ability. When the meeting broke, Jim Coman asked if I had any questions. I did not but I was feeling good about how things went.

The second meeting with the special prosecutors did not go nearly as well. This time other people were in the room. There were four white males and one white female. Later a black woman joined us. The three white men were identified as members of the State Bureau of Investigation (SBI).

The extra people in the room made me especially uncomfortable. I was not expecting such a large gathering and the demeanor of those watching did not make me feel they were on my side. We all sat around a large conference table. There was an easel set up; I was given a long pointing stick and asked to go over the events of the night of March 13 while the people in the room stared at me. I was visibly uncomfortable. I struggled with my words and felt confused at times because I could not stand the looks I was getting. I was told I needed to describe again in detail what had happened. It was excruciating and humiliating, trying to tell my story to people who were visibly hostile.

I had prepared myself for what I thought was going to be a strategy session on the case. Instead it felt like I was on the witness stand trying to defend myself. After about two hours, I was reduced to tears and was forced to stop. During our break for lunch, I completely lost my composure. I cried uncontrollably. One of the SBI agents suggested that I get some fresh air and I might feel better. I did not want to go out of the room and be seen as a basket case.

The lone black female appeared and went with me to the bathroom. I talked with the woman for some time and felt better. When everyone returned to the conference room, I thought I had myself together enough to improve my presentation. I still believed that everyone there was on the side of justice. Had I known what was coming next, I would have had my own attorney with me.

Jim Coman launched into a series of rapid-fire questions. "Where were you raped? Which door did you enter and exit? Were they the same doors? Did Mr. Nifong tell you the names of your attackers?"

I felt like I had answered all those questions a dozen times already. Mr. Coman's delivery of the questions seemed designed to frustrate me. Maybe he was getting me ready for being on the stand, but it was still painful. I started to cry again. I could not take it anymore and left the room in tears. I went to the bathroom escorted by Mary Winstead and the lady who had comforted me the first time.

Mary Winstead put her arm around me and spoke, "We have to make sure, understand? We are preparing you for a trial so hang in there. Okay?"

I dried my eyes, and I know it must have seemed like I was a complete wreck. This was tough and I was having a hard time believing that this was for my benefit. When we started Jim Coman "lit" into me from all directions. I was as frustrated as I was scared. Why was not someone on my side in this? I had met with the police and Mike Nifong and never once did I feel like I was not being respected.

The others in the room sat by and did not intervene. Not once did anyone say, "We don't believe you." At least if they said that I would have been clear on where they were coming from. I would have understood this meeting for what it was, a way to tell the world that I was crazy and delusional. I did grow increasingly frustrated and agitated. I could not hold back any longer and I blurted out what I felt. "They are going to get away with it because Duke has paid everyone to be silent." It was not the smartest thing for me to do. I did not know what else to say at that point. It was my word against everything the defense attorneys had been able to amass. I thought that maybe the special prosecutors were convinced that I was deranged because of what they had been hearing in the media.

Leaving the meeting I still had no sense that the case was soon going to be over. A year had passed and it was apparent I was right back where I had started. How many times would I have to recount my story before I could just make it to court and get on the witness stand? Even after that meeting, I imagined that we were headed for a trial.

With the release of the attorney general's report in April 2007, it was all over for the people who had been charged. They held their celebrations and collected their settlement checks. I was left to wonder what happened. Roy Cooper, the North Carolina attorney general, made the unprecedented proclamation that someone was "innocent." As I read through the report, I thought, "Is this what I waited so long for? What about my rights?" I thought that if they did not want to pursue rape charges they could move forward. If nothing else, there should have been enough evidence to prove that racial slurs where used during the assault. I could not dwell on what I could not change. I would have to refocus my energy on getting my life together.

I did feel sorry for Mike Nifong. Now that the defense lawyers had the report in hand, they were free to go about getting as much money as they could from anyone they could sue. With his law license gone, Mike Nifong was vulnerable. He had served Durham for a long time and now on account of me, he was going to have to pay with his career. It did not seem fair and I believe the majority of people who think rationally know what the North Carolina Bar did was well beyond what was necessary or had ever been done in the past. Nevertheless, the forces aligned against the case needed

Nifong's license or there would be no grounds for the lawsuits that were to come.

I would have to listen to more talk about me being some crazy, drug-crazed hooker for another entire year. Pulling myself out of the funk that I was in was done through pure determination. This was just another bump in the road and not the end of the line. The one thing I knew I had to do was to finish college. After all, I had been dancing to pay for school and taking care of the kids. If I could not dance, the kids still needed to be taken care of. The only way I was going to get a job was to have a degree and some marketable skills. It was time to forgive and forget. If North Carolina said the case was closed, then it was closed. If the individuals who had been charged were said to be innocent, then they were innocent. I did not have the time or resources to prove otherwise.

I am left with hating the way it felt to be accused of being something I was not. So, of course I felt badly if any of the people charged were not held responsible for making my life a living hell. Nobody should believe for a moment that I wanted to hurt innocent people. It is not in my nature, and I reject any characterizations that portray me as wanting to somehow harm people for my own benefit.

New Beginning

With the writing of this book, my healing process begins. Whether I can go on with my life will not be important to most people, but it is to me because I plan to go on, be productive, and offer better chances for my children. I believe I have to find healing for myself. I also want to provide healing for those who feel they have been hurt. I know there are many people who are suffering from some kind of trauma and my story may provide a point of common ground where they can start their process of reconciliation. I can only talk about my life. The good, the bad, and the ugly parts have been what I have lived and they have brought me to this place in time. I know how each moment of the life I have lived has had an impact on who and what I am today.

Others have tried to tell my story for me, but they do not have that right. Only I have that right and, due to the circumstances, I believe I have that responsibility to try to set the record straight about a lot of things. I have had to endure almost two years of constant negative talk about my life by people who were only trying to hurt and discredit me. It is as though my life was destined to be intertwined with Durham, NCCU, and Duke University. My family and I had been patients at the world-renowned Duke University Medical Center several times throughout our lives and so there will always be a connection to Duke. My sister graduated from NCCU, and proudly I have too. I graduated with honors and earned every point of my GPA.

Everyone knows that Duke is a place to get a great education. As much as people know about Duke they know little or nothing about my alma mater. North Carolina Central University is the home of the Eagles and was founded in 1909. It accepted its first students in 1910. Back then it was known as The National Religious Training School and Chautauqua. By 1923 the school started receiving support from the state and became the Durham State Normal School. One of the great ironies—Benjamin Newton Duke was one of the school's early benefactors. He is the same person who would grant money to Trinity College, which would later rename itself Duke University in his family's honor.

Duke and NCCU share a past in playing some of the first interracial college basketball games in the South, even though it was under the cover of darkness and in secret. That occurred when NCCU was the much better team. The Eagles produced some of the greatest athletes in all sports in this country.

The law school at NCCU, while not as renowned as its cross-town cousin, is consistently ranked as one of the best small law schools in the United States and is recognized as a great place for women to attend. It has also produced a governor of North Carolina, Mike Easley, and many of the state's top lawmakers and politicians.

Overall NCCU has been a great institution and produced many outstanding graduates. I felt I had to say something about that because my school has been the subject of bad press because of what people think about me.

I know the people at NCCU tried to show the better side of the university when they had a chance, but they never should have been put in a position to have to do that in the first place. The story became about everything it was not supposed to be. The students at NCCU who came out in support of me were not asking for anything other than to let the system work the case out. Instead they had to endure some of the same treatment that I got. I am sorry the people who had nothing to do with the case were dragged into the middle of it.

Has anyone stopped to think that I did not start the media frenzy? Why would I challenge the reputation, money, and resources that Duke University possesses? Would anyone make up this incident in some misguided and elaborate plan to sue Duke, as some have postulated in the blogs and on some irresponsible media outlets?

I wondered why the media did not add a qualifier to the description of the people who hosted the party. Why not say they were drunken, out-of-control party boys? There was a criminal case going on and the court is the place where things should be decided, not on Hannity and Colmes.

Additionally, I believe in the rape shield laws. It would not have made any sense for me to go public because I believed that it put too much strain on a person who is already traumatized. It was hard enough to go through this in private and alone. Just imagine if I had made appearances on television trying to explain my side of the story. I would have been eaten alive and suffered even harsher ridicule. I was engaged in activities and living in a lifestyle that few people would approve or would understand. It is true that the people you hang around with will influence what others think about you. I was hanging around people who did not mean me well. Despite those true things, I wanted everyone to know the real me. No news outlet on their own was going to look for the real me.

Now that there has been almost two years since the case began, I can read with a new perspective some of the characterizations of me. My first reaction is always to be angry. The things that were said about my background, my school, and my city were hurtful. What I have found there is hardly a flattering description of any aspects of my life.

So without any reservations or hesitation, I define myself as a mother, student, and daughter before all else. I know others have descriptions of me that are not anything I would use to describe myself.

As I think about some of the people who made it a point to hurt me, one of the greatest disappointments is to know that there were people in my own community undermining me and creating the worst rumors. One was a prominent Durham attorney and sports agent who said about me, "C'mon, kids. She wasn't this little poor North Carolina Central student working the fields. She was a whore."

I was not disappointed because he is a big-time lawyer and respected in the community. It did not matter that he was black or from Durham. I was disappointed because he asks people to give his clients the benefit of the doubt all the time. He wants to set aside the records of the criminal defendants he represents so that they get a fair trial. This is the same attorney who was on the defense team helping to represent Michael Vick and served on the team of attorneys for some of the Duke Lacrosse players.

This attorney turned out to be representing one of the men who produced a videotape allegedly showing me dancing days after the party. The only problem is the tape was from months before the events of March 13, 2006. CBS and other media outlets played the tape over and over. It found a home on the Internet. People argue to this day that the tape somehow proves that I am a liar. Even though people now know better, they have never wanted to go back and correct that kind of attack on me.

So I was supposed to remain silent forever and let everyone else have the last word about me? I freely admit that the jobs I was paid to do are not what I want my daughters to grow up and do. I cannot recommend exotic dancing to be anyone's first choice for a profession. Because of a serious mistake that I made in the past, my job options were limited and I worked in an industry that does not help a person build a stellar reputation.

There were and still are many Web sites and blogs that purport to know every detail about my life, spelling it out authoritatively with charts, graphs, and timelines, but have no compulsion to check the facts. Those people have anointed themselves the repository of official information about me. I talked to only one media outlet about my life and that was very early on in the case. It was an act that I regret very much doing. I did not realize at the time that it was probably best not to say anything at all. Samiha Khanna of *The N&O* said she wanted to help me, and that telling my story to her and her colleagues would help bring the people who hurt me to justice. The information I provided to *The N&O* was only a sketch of my life. I never could have really detailed all the aspects of my life when I gave them limited access through my screen door.

It was not until I began writing down my thoughts that I even thought about some of the things that have happened in my life. It would be much later before I would sit down for extended recorded interviews. After my experience with *The N&O*, I refused to talk to anyone because I could never trust any of the people who said they wanted to help me.

The only time I purposely tried to get my side of the story out to the public was well after the attorney general's report. I allowed CNN to come interview me and spend time with my family in January 2008. I let them follow me to class, come to my church, and even videotape my children. We even sat down for a four-hour interview in a hotel suite near the Raleigh-Durham Airport. There I allowed Soledad O'Brien to ask me whatever questions she wanted. I had nothing to hide and believed if people finally saw and heard me, I could finish the process of making this part of my life truly a part of my past.

Throughout the entire process of working with CNN, I felt they were disappointed that I was not a drug addict and on welfare. They had the opportunity to see me and the people around me, but they would never talk to anyone I mentioned to them or put anyone I suggested in front of the camera. It was as though they did not want to hear from anyone else—my pastor, my professors, my advisors, and experts on North Carolina law that I knew were not important to CNN. I was honest and candid in the interview, but apparently it was not good enough.

After allowing them into personal life and my home, someone at CNN decided this reporting was not something they wanted the public to see. I had even let them read an early manuscript of this book, but they have refused to share with me any of the video footage they shot of me and my family. I was used again. Now, when I call CNN, no one will take my call. They have nothing to say about what they saw. When I asked why the footage was not going to be shown, I received no answer.

In a world where there is wall-to-wall coverage of the Peterson case or of Natalie Holloway, surely there was a place to show my interview. Even if they did not believe a word I said, they were not protecting me by not showing it. I believe they were protecting other people. If I am not crazy and on drugs, then many of the things other people have said about me are open to liable and slander suits. I'm not the least bit concerned about any of the footage being shown. I presented my life as an open book.

The entire process of working with CNN was not negative. The cameramen, producers, and Soledad O'Brien were all nice to me. Everyone was professional and they went about their work in a serious manner. What I have concerns about is what was the real motivation for spending all that time and money to interview me if it was never going to be aired.

My suspicion is that people who have an interest in the civil cases feel that any portrait of me that is *not* negative will have a harmful effect on their suits in reference to Duke University and the city of Durham. Not airing the program was one more poke in the eye for me. Another attempt to work in good faith with someone and then to be let down again.

Another aspect of the telling of my story by the media and the bloggers that bothers me is their portrayal of the city of Durham. The stories made it seem as though there was so much racial tension as a result of the case that the city was under siege. Durham is like any other city in America with a significant black population. There are always factions within a city who attempt to care for their own interests. Groups in Durham such as the Committee on the Affairs of Black People have existed since black people were not able to muster enough political or economic power to improve their condition because of overt racism. North Carolina has had to deal with the legacy of segregation and Jim Crow.

Durham has had to transform itself after the death of the tobacco industry that once flourished in the town. The Lucky Strike Tower is the centerpiece of the new downtown revitalization. It was with tobacco money that the city of Durham came into being. It was also cheap black labor that made the industry profitable. The construction of the Durham Freeway did substantial damage to the solidarity and prosperity of the black community.

Durham gets singled out as a community with high crime and bad place to live—these are the Durham working-class people that I come from.

I have experienced the kind of life I do not want for my children or anyone else. I do not want to be remembered as a troubled girl, who ends up being a troubled woman, who ends up saddling her troubled life on the backs of her children and grandchildren. Being the matriarch of a dysfunctional family is a terrible legacy that many women of all races have to live with.

While my story has components of race in it, there are multiple narratives dealing with more than race. However, I am not afraid to acknowledge that the motivation on the part of some who participated in discrediting me was racist.

Perhaps the telling of my story will give us an opportunity to discuss racism calmly.

There are also clearly issues of sexism that exist in my story. Many have criticized my choice to be a dancer but find it hard to condemn men who use women for entertainment. This is despite the fact that men conceived of and hosted the kind of party that had all the elements of bad taste, alcohol abuse, racial animosity, and a sexually charged environment that could lead to nothing but trouble.

Being in the public eye and under so much scrutiny has been difficult. Even as I try to move on with my life, I still find it necessary to take one more stand and fight. I want to assert, without equivocation, that I was assaulted. Make of that what you will. You will decide what that means to you because the state of North Carolina saw fit not to look at all that happened the night I became infamous.

When I spoke, I was accused of changing my story repeatedly. I emphasize now that the story has never changed. The fact is I did not make it to court to state my case because the focus became one of discrediting me and exposing my personal life instead of finding the truth. So I am left to defend myself. I am not looking forward to opening old wounds. I have never in my life intended to hurt anyone; it is the same with me telling you about my life and what happened at 610 North Buchanan.

You already know a lot about me. More than I ever wanted people to know. On account of this incident I have shared with you some things from my past that are very difficult to talk about but necessary. I am not trying to please everyone, but perhaps I can finally please myself.

For all the women who have been beaten by their partners and labeled battered women, for those like me who will forever be despised and dismissed as just someone who made up things, I am writing this book. I am also writing for those women who have been labeled accusers like me, women who may have not been able to move forward with their lives because of the double violation that they had to suffer—once at the hands of their attacker and then at the hands of the institutions that have the power to ruin lives and enrich others at the stroke of a pen.

So, when I walked across the stage at graduation to receive my degree at NCCU, I knew I was finally putting what had happened behind me. The whole reason why I was at that party in the first place was to pay my tuition. Here I was graduating with honors, and I did not need to dance to accomplish my goal. That is the lesson I learned. There are no short cuts.

On account of what has happened to me, I feel more inspired. I am working as hard as I ever have to help my children grow up to be better people and contribute positively to society. I will show others that there is a way out of misery and an easier path to take to a happier life. If you stumble, it does not mean you will fall. My dreams, my heartache, and my desire to carry on have become the basis for my strength.

Epilogue

When I started this project, I had one goal in mind. That was to make sure people heard from Crystal. I have been distressed that very few have been able to see how destructive the coverage of this tragedy has been. The coverage had not just been one-sided; the tone was just plain mean-spirited. I know I am not unique in my view of the world. Something was completely out of balance.

All of the major religions talk about redemption, atonement, and forgiveness. This is one of those cases that beg for us to evoke all of those principles and then some. However, being able to look at this case from the vantage point that would allow a person to "move on" requires some rational thinking. Rational thinking has been very scarce in the case, and I fear that we may be too far past the time to ask people to think and reason.

I believe that something happened at 610 North Buchanan Boulevard. I don't know what that is nor what to call it. Nonetheless, I also believe the only way to know the truth is to lay all of the cards on the table. That first begins by letting Crystal speak for herself. Because there is no longer a criminal case and there is no threat of prosecution, I wish people would just stop with all of the threats of civil action.

Everyone else has had their say. That has been impossible for Crystal up to this point due to several reasons. First and foremost there was no forum that would allow her to speak. So, I created one in the form of this book. Second, she is under constant threat for her life, her family's safety and her ability to make living has been severely hampered. Imagine what it is like to not knowing if you can go to sleep safely at night. Added to that is the constant threat of being sued. The stress of not wanting to be in public because it would make you a target is unfair and not necessary.

I know the argument is that the defendants in the case and all of the lacrosse players were harmed because they faced possible prison time. Every person ever arrested for any reason has faced some punishment. The truth is facing punishment is not the same as actually spending years of your life in jail. I have been arrested for something I did not do, and that arrest follows me everywhere I go. I have to explain it time and time again.

Nevertheless, how then can you reach a state of peace in your heart and mind when you feel not a single soul is willing to listen with an open mind or consider to "let sleeping dogs lie." No one in this case has faced any real serious threat to his or her life other than Crystal. I fear the same thing for myself since taking up this cause. I know that people believe their lives were ruined, but if we are completely honest, everyone is much better off then they were the night of March 13, 2006. All have grown, become more mature, and would hopefully never put themselves in the same situation ever again.

I cannot fool myself into expecting that Crystal and I will not be crucified for daring to speak. It is not a new concept to drag your enemy through the mud. There always has to be winners and losers. People just do not like it any other way. What I do wish for is rational discourse on all of the significant issues that arose from this case. As I prepare to move on with my life, I can only hope that Crystal and everyone involved in this can have some peace when they go to bed tonight and every night from this moment on. There should be a time when this case does not evoke the strongest emotions we have, like hate and vengefulness.

I can tell you without a doubt that Crystal does not harbor any resentment towards anyone. She is the single most reasonable person I have ever discussed the concept of atonement with. She has always been the one to see a positive point in this utterly bad situation. I wish others had the capacity to be so generous in the ability to forgive and have the capacity to find a silver lining.

Too many people took this case as justification for their own cause and failed to look at all of the uncontrollable forces that were at work. This case has been about race, sex, class, prosecutorial discretion, and morality all at the same time. There is too much in it to be wrapped up in a neat package. But I beg people to allow this to be the last word on the matter.

Finally, I still cannot believe how much attention the case received. Despite the murkiness of this case, the most curious group to take it up as a cause was the right-wing ideologues. They have from the outset tried to define this case as some litmus test on the judicial system. The odd part is they have never once expressed any concern about how criminal cases are prosecuted for the poor or minorities. Everyday, hundreds of defendants stand in the dock and protest their innocence and the right has had little tolerance for things like Open File Discovery and the timely release of evidence that might be viewed as exculpatory. Why then, in this case where people are such law and order types, do they want so much to punish anyone associated with the prosecution?

I believe it has everything to do with the race and status of the defendants. I am suggesting that it does not matter one bit whether or not anything happened at 610 North Buchanan. The loudest critics would have lined up on the side for exoneration—no matter what—because the defendants were not poor and not black. That is a harsh assessment, but I have little choice but to believe it. These people have never expressed the slightest concern for people seeking exoneration if they are poor or black.

Does that mean that I believe there would have been convictions for assault and first degree kidnapping had this case gone to trial? No, not necessarily. The outcome may have been the same as what the attorney general found. What I am suggesting is that the forces who lined up to support the tactics of the defense would never have taken up the cause had these been black Duke football players. My suggestion is based on the fact that the loudest voices on the case have come from the group that constantly vilifies trial lawyers and believes in being tough on crime. The quote from Shakespeare's "The Tempest" goes, "Misery acquaints a man with strange bedfellows." This case fits Shakespeare's observation precisely. This is a miserable situation. The bedfellows in this case are the right-wing hit men and liberal trial lawyers like Joe Cheshire and Brad Bannon—strange bedfellows, indeed.

What very few people know about the Duke Lacrosse case is that it has a very strong connection to the exoneration of black and poor defendants sitting on the death row in North Carolina. At the same time the Duke Lacrosse players needed defense attorneys, the defense attorneys needed another case to help push through legislation on the rules of discovery in criminal cases. This could get to be overwhelming for some people to follow, but it is extremely important to understand if you want to know why North Carolina Attorney General Roy Cooper had to create an entirely new legal definition, "Innocent of all charges."

Joe Cheshire and his law partners are famous in North Carolina. They have for years been the consummate trial lawyers because they have taken on the state in cases that nobody else is willing or able to take. They have managed to hand North Carolina a staggering number of defeats. Their clients tend to get off. Most recently, the trial lawyers have even been winning in death row appeal cases too. This group of defense lawyers is adept at achieving exonerations because district attorneys lied or made evidence appear to be something it was not.

We should applaud the efforts of lawyers like Cheshire who have been fighting for truth and justice for the little man. Joe Cheshire is without a doubt a champion of that cause. Consequently, he would be described by most on the right as a liberal, a leader of the trial lawyers, and staunch opponent of the death penalty. His family has prided itself on being a leader in the civil rights struggle. One fact he likes to point out is that his family was instrumental in founding the historically black Episcopal college, Saint Augustine's in Raleigh. He is also always eager to share his encounter with Dr. Martin Luther King, Jr. when he was in his early teens. King is one of Joe Cheshire's heroes.

The biggest irony is that much of what the defense lawyers were able to achieve by winning exoneration in the Duke case will aid groups like the ACLU and NAACP in cases such as that of James Johnson in Wilson, North Carolina. If you are not familiar with that case, you should be. I challenge everyone who wants to put this case to rest to take the time to look at what has been happening in North Carolina with exonerations over the past five years. The Duke Lacrosse case was not an anomaly.

I believe the real legacy of the Duke case will be that the state of North Carolina will free many poor and minority men that have been wrongly accused. They will also have to free some criminals as well. Because, as Joe Cheshire has pointed out for years, the biggest problems with criminal defense in North Carolina courts has to do with ineptness of counsel as much as rogue prosecution.

If there is one shred of good that can come from this, we should take advantage of it. Today, take the time to forgive someone. Do not hold on to hate or require vengefulness to feel whole. In the words of Frances Bacon, "Grace is getting something that you don't deserve; and mercy is not getting something that you do deserve." Crystal's brief performance on North Buchanan Boulevard was indeed her last dance for grace.

Printed in the United States
214639BV00001B/1/P